ENOCHIAN SEX MAGIC
AND HOW TO WORKBOOK

Some Other Titles From New Falcon Publications

Aha! The Sevenfold Mystery of the Ineffable Love —Aleister Crowley
Bio-Etheric Healing —Trudy Lanitis
Undoing Yourself With Energized Meditation and Other Devices
Secrets of Western Tantra: The Sexuality of the Middle Path
Dogma Daze —Christopher S. Hyatt, Ph.D.
Rebels & Devils; The Psychology of Liberation–Edited by Christopher S. Hyatt, Ph.D.
Aleister Crowley's Illustrated Goetia
Sex Magic, Tantra & Tarot: The Way of the Secret Lover
Taboo: Sex, Religion & Magick —C. Hyatt, Ph.D., and DuQuette
Pacts With The Devil, Urban Voodoo: A Beginner's Guide to Afro-Caribbean Magic
—Jason Black and Christopher S. Hyatt, Ph.D.
The Psychopath's Bible —Christopher S. Hyatt, Ph.D., and Jack Willis
Ask Baba Lon —Lon Milo DuQuette
Aleister Crowley and the Treasure House of Images
–J.F.C. Fuller, Aleister Crowley, Lon Milo DuQuette and Nancy Wasserman
Enochian Sex Magic and How To Workbook
—Aleister Crowley, Lon Milo DuQuette and Christopher S. Hyatt, Ph.D.
Enochian World of Aleister Crowley —DuQuette and Aleister Crowley
Info-Psychology, Neuropolitique, The Game of Life, What Does WoMan Want?
—Timothy Leary, Ph.D.
Rebellion, Revolution and Religiousness —Osho
Reichian Therapy: A Practical Guide for Home Use —Dr. Jack Willis
Woman's Orgasm: A Guide to Sexual Satisfaction
—Benjamin Graber, M.D., and Georgia Kline-Graber, R.N.
Shaping Formless Fire
Seizing Power
Taking Power —Stephen Mace
The Illuminati Conspiracy: The Sapiens System —Donald Holmes, M.D.
An Insider's Guide to Robert Anton Wilson —Eric Wagner
The Secret Inner Order Rituals of the Golden Dawn —Pat Zalewski
Nonlocal Nature: The Eight Circuits of Consciousness –James A. Heffernan
on What is —Ja Wallin

Other Titles by J. Marvin Spiegelman, Ph.D.

A Modern Jew in Search of Soul
Buddhism and Jungian Psychology
Catholicism and Jungian Psychology
Hinduism and Jungian Psychology
Mysticism, Psychology and Oedipus - A Small Gem
Protestanism and Jungian Psychology
Psychotherapy and Religion at the Millennium and Beyond
Psychotherapy as a Mutual Process
Reich, Jung, Regardie & Me - The Unhealed Healer
Rider, Haggard, Henry Miller & I - The Unpublished Writer
Sufism, Islam and Jungian Psychology
The Knight - A Small Gem
The Nymphomaniac
The Quest - Further Adventures in the Unconscious
The Tree of Life - Paths in Jungian Individuation
The Wisdom of J. Marvin Speigelman Vol. I - Selected Writings
The Wisdom of J. Marvin Speigelman Vol. II - Psychology and Religion

Other Titles by Dr. Israel Regardie

A Garden of Pomegranates
A Practical Guide to Geomantic Divination - A Small Gem
Attract and Use Healing Energy - A Small Gem
Be Yourself - A Guide to Relaxation and Health
Ceremonial Magic
Dr. Israel Regardie's Definitive Work on Aleister Crowley,
    The Eye In The Triangle
Healing Energy, Prayer and Relaxation
How To Make and Use Talismans - A Small Gem
My Rosicrucian Adventure
Mysticism, Psychology and Oedipus - A Small Gem
Teachers of Fulfillment
The Art and Meaning of Magic - A Small Gem
The Body-Mind Connection, A Path to Well-Being - A Small Gem
The Complete Golden Dawn System of Magic
The Complete Golden Dawn System of Magic Book 1 - Ltd. Edition
The Complete Golden Dawn System of Magic Book 2 - Ltd. Edition
The Complete Golden Dawn System of Magic - The Black Edition
The Eye in the Triangle: An Interpretation of Aleister Crowley
The Golden Dawn Audio CDs, Vol. 1, Vol. 2, and Vol. 3
The Legend of Aleister Crowley
The Magic of Israel Regardie
The Middle Pillar
The Philosopher's Stone
The Portable Complete Golden Dawn System of Magic
The Tree of Life
The Wisdom of Israel Regardie - Vol. I
    Selected Introductions, Prefaces and Forewords
The Wisdom of Israel Regardie - Vol. II
    Selected Essays and Commentaries
The Wisdom of Israel Regardie - Vol. III
    Selected Articles, Introductions, Prefaces and Forewords
What You Should Know About the Golden Dawn
Wilhelm Reich, His Theory And Techniques
Aha! (Dr. Israel Regardie and Aleister Crowley)
Roll Away The Stone/The Herb Dangerous
    (Dr. Israel Regardie and Aleister Crowley)

MANY OF OUR TITLES AVAILABLE ON KINDLE!
Please visit our website at http://www.newfalcon.com

Copyright © 1991 U.S.E.S.S.
United States Ecclesiastical Society and Seminary

All rights reserved. No part of this book, in part or in whole, may be reproduced, transmitted, or utilized, in any form or by any means, electronic or mechanical, including photocopying, recording, or by any information storage and retrieval system, without permission in writing from the publisher, except for brief quotations in critical articles, books and reviews.

ISBN 10: 1-56184-543-4
ISBN 13: 978-1-56184-543-9

First Edition 1991
Second Printing 1993
Third Printing 1997
Fourth Printing 2002
Fifth Printing 2005
Sixth Printing 2006
Second Revised Edition 2011
Third Revised Edition 2021
Ninth Printing 2022

The paper used in this publication meets the minimum requirements of the American National Standard for Permanence of Paper for Printed Library Materials Z39.48-1984

Printed in USA

NEW FALCON PUBLICATIONS
2046 Hillhurst Avenue
Los Angeles, CA 90027
www.newfalcon.com
email: info@newfalcon.com

ENOCHIAN SEX MAGIC
AND HOW TO WORKBOOK

ALEISTER CROWLEY
LON MILO DuQUETTE
CHRISTOPHER S. HYATT, PH.D.

With New Prologue by Lon Milo DuQuette

Sex Magic Symbols Illustrated By
David P. Wilson

NEW FALCON PUBLICATIONS
Los Angeles, California

Table of Contents

Prologue
By Lon Milo DuQuette, 2021 — ix

Foreword
By Christopher S. Hyatt, Ph.D., 1991 — xiii

Introduction
By Lon Milo DuQuette, 1991 — xvii

Chapter One
A Short, Brief History (Abridged) — 1

Chapter Two
Before We Start Let's Get Something Straight — 3

Chapter Three
The Ten Minute Overview — 5

Chapter Four
Comments on Liber LXXXIV vel Chanokh — 11

Chapter Five
Liber LXXXIV vel Chanokh — 35

Chapter Six
Divine Eroticism — 73

Chapter Seven
Techniques Of Enochian Sex Magick — 79

Chapter Eight
The Enochian Dictionary — 93

Appendix I
The Enochian Calls (Keys) — 111

Appendix II
The Enochian Diagrams — 127

Appendix III
The Lesser Rituals of the Pentagram and Hexagram — 139

Sex Magic Symbols — 143

Pattern for Enochian Square — 151

Dedicted To
MASTER THERION
CONSTANCE AND JEAN-PAUL
GARY AND CINDY

Prologue
to the 2021 Edition

by Lon Milo DuQuette

Enochian Magick has been the centerpiece of my private magical practice and public teaching for forty years. I prefer teaching this kind of magick in a 'workshop' setting, because I believe it is the fastest, most painless, and most effective way to wholesomely addict the new student to a magical 'obsession'—an obsession with the colorful and elegant imagery of cascading cosmic fractals of infinitely repeating and permuting patterns of consciousness, human and divine...patterns that build (upward/downward/inward/outward) one-upon another, one-within another to form choirs angelic hierarchies forces and energies drive the dynamo of consciousness that is the Elemental universe. No other magical system, in my opinion, does a better job of drawing-in and involving the magician within this machinery of consciousness than Enochian magick.

In Chapter Four of this little book, I make the suggestion that the reader make his or her own set of Enochian Elemental Tablets by photographically enlarging and printing out copies of Plates IV, V, VI, VII and VIII and carefully coloring them in a precise step-by-step manner. Actually, I'm stating unequivocally…if you truly are serious about absorbing the essence of Enochian Magick (even at this beginning level) you should really create your own colored set of Elemental Tablets (including the small Tablet of Union).

Following the book's step-by-step instructions for this (almost pre-school level) art project will magically educate you more than hundreds of hours of reading, study and memorization. Furthermore, you will be subjectively programing your psyche (through the medium of the cones and rods of your own eyes) with the elemental structure of the cosmos itself; and be rewarded with a beautiful (and magically 'charged') set of Enochian Elemental Tablets suitable as magical tools for your subsequent visionary work with the Enochian system.

Crowley, and adepts of the Golden Dawn imagined each lettered square of the Tablet of Union and the four Elemental Tablets as being the flattened 'apex' of a three dimensional, four-sided pyramid–each side painted the appropriate elemental color. By simply looking at a flat version of the tablets one can easily imagine what a three dimensional set of tablets would look like. Early in my Enochian studies I wanted to create a colorful three-dimensional set of tablets. I called my mentor, Israel Regardie, and told him I was anxious to start the project and he said something to the effect of, 'Oh dear boy! That sounds like a real pain! Besides, the tablets can be dangerous enough when they are flat. Don't give the little buggers dimensional room to manifest!.'

I wasn't certain if he were joking or not, but allowing the Enochian spirits to 'manifest' was pretty much what I wanted to have happen. I politely ignored his cautious advice and went ahead and constructed my own set of wooden, three-dimensional tablets. I have never regretted doing so. I encourage the reader (if you are serious about the art of

Enochian Magick) to create your own three-dimensional tablets (at very least the Tablet of Union). You will learn so much in the process and in a subtle way implant the 'code' of Enochian Magick deep in your psyche. I have included after Appendix III of this book a simple form for creating a truncated pyramid (page 121) that you can reproduce and print out on card stock. (You will need only twenty of them to make a beautiful Tablet of Union).

Over the years I have received many positive comments about this little book. I have used it for 28 years as a handbook and workbook for my Enochian classes and workshops. I have always hoped that subsequent editions would include the word "Workbook" to the title–for that is precisely what it is.

Lon Milo DuQuette

Foreword
by Christopher S. Hyatt, Ph.D.
1991

How do you know when you are really beginning to understand a subject?

When you come to the realization that it is basically much easier than you ever imagined.

For years I avoided an in-depth study of Enochian Magick, believing it to be not only too ponderous a task but also anachronistically irrelevant. I considered it a quaint dead-end of Elizabethan magic, elements of which have trickled down the centuries and lodged themselves in modern ceremonial magic.

I admit that I had a certain level of curiosity and fascination, especially when I saw the painted tablets and Enochian "chess" equipment that Israel Regardie would display on rare occasions to his friends. But the idea of actually taking the time to make sense of this collection of complex and fragmentary material was totally intimidating. And the thought of having to learn an "angelic language" did not thrill me at all. I was quite happy to file Enochian Magick in the same drawer of my mind where I kept *Secrets of Aztec Cardiology*" and *"Cooking with Barbed Wire."* Then several years ago I was pleasantly disabused.

I had asked Crowley expert, Lon DuQuette, to write an epilogue for my book, *Secrets of Western Tantra*, (Falcon Press, 1989) and in the course of our discussion he asked me if I had ever utilized Enochian Angels for operations of Sex Magick. He was genuinely amused when I revealed my reasons for avoiding the subject and he suggested that if ever I wished to learn how to immediately perform Enochian Magick, I should simply read Crowley's *Liber Chanokh* and get started.

When I protested that I had read it, that in fact, it was included in *Gems From the Equinox*, (Falcon Press, 1982). He said, "then read it again, carefully, and this time assume that everything you need to know is right there in the text."

He continued. "It is much simpler than you think." He then encouraged me to call him if I ran into trouble.

His somewhat cavalier attitude was oddly reassuring, so I took some time that evening to reread *Chanokh*. I followed his advice and pretended it was the only book on the subject in the world. To my great surprise I discovered that everything seemed quite clear. Was this the same book that frustrated and confused me earlier? Did I all of a sudden become so much smarter? Questions that were raised by one sentence were answered in the next. The fundamentals of the system unfolded neatly before my eyes. In less than an hour, I felt perfectly competent to start basic operations. I had no reason to call Lon for advice.

When I did call him it was to tell him of my application of the system to elements of my Tantric practices and that I wished to publish *Chanokh* along with his comments and supplementary material of my own findings. I have enjoyed our collaboration very much for his enthusiasm for the subject has been irresistibly contagious. Now we invite you to enter *The Enochian World of Aleister Crowley*.

Relax. It is much simpler than you think and I guarantee you that if you do embark upon the sexual practices all of your efforts will be well rewarded.

Introduction
by Lon Milo DuQuette
1991

In the introduction of a recently published book on magick, the writer characterizes the Enochian material in Crowley's *Equinox* as being "scanty" and in "disarray". I am afraid I could not disagree more. In fact, it is so exquisitely comprehensive and laid out with such orderly neatness that, (to quote Masonic scholar, Gary Ford), "Crowley can only be criticized for being too anal retentive."

If the critic was capable of paying attention and spent the hour or less that it takes to read *Chanokh* she couldn't help but grasp the subject. This, is my opinion, cannot be said of any other text on the subject.

For example, the somewhat complex explanation of how the 18 Calls are ordered and combined for invocations of the 16 different sub angles takes four pages in Regardie's Complete *Golden Dawn System Of Magic*, (Falcon Press, 1984). Crowley does it easily in *10 seconds*.

I will not argue that Crowley demands much from his readers. But in the case of *Liber LXXXIV vel Chanokh* the difficulty is that one finds it almost impossible to believe that so much is communicated in so few words.

> ***The genuineness of these Keys, altogether apart from any critical observation, is guaranteed by the fact that anyone with the smallest capacity for Magick finds that they work.***
>
> *Aleister Crowley*

Twenty five years ago few members of the general occult community had ever heard of the Enochian system of Magick. Those who were aware of its existence fell into two main categories:

I. Members of the surviving magical societies which operated in the basic traditions of **Ordo Templi Orientis, A∴A∴** or **The Golden Dawn.**

II. Individuals lucky enough to possess either of two long-out-of-print works:
The Equinox Volume I, Numbers 7 & 8
The Golden Dawn Volumes 1-4

The Equinox, Aleister Crowley's Magnum Opus, issued at six month intervals between 1909 and 1914, was the first modern publication to examine the Enochian system in the seventh and eighth books of the ten number series.

Israel Regardie's *Account Of The Teachings, Rites and Ceremonies Of The Golden Dawn* followed in four volumes, the first published in 1937 and the fourth in 1940.

Though material relating directly to Enochiana occupies only a fraction of the above texts, the quality of the material is unquestioned. Both provide clear fundamental information that gives the student both a basic understanding of the system and all the tools necessary to begin to immediately apply it and operate Enochian Magick.

In 1969 Regardie's *Golden Dawn* was reissued in a two volume format and then in 1974 he edited and released *Gems From The Equinox* containing all the Enochian material from the original 10 volume set. Both works are still in print. *The Complete Golden Dawn System of Magic*, (Falcon Press, 1984) Regardie's tour de force published shortly before his death, includes his invaluable, *Addendum to the Concourse of Forces*. This tome stands as a monument to both the man and the material. This time the Enochian Genii has stayed out of the bottle.

Since 1969 an increasing number of students have turned their attention to this attractive yet, at first glance, overwhelmingly complex system. Their diligence is rewarded with something very rare indeed–a magical system that really works!

This takes many arm-chair magicians entirely off guard. A legitimate encounter with an Elemental Spirit or an Angel of an Æthyr invariably leaves a more lasting impression on the magician than the phantoms of self-deluded wishing thinking that mark the "successful working" of the dilettante.

Today Enochiana commands a respectable amount of space on the shelves of your local occult or New Age bookstore. Much of the original Dee material (still existent) has been reprinted and made available to an ever-growing body of readers. The students of the early 1970s have become the researchers and prolific authors of today.

Many of the new works are excellent and offer invaluable contributions to the ever-increasing library of Enochian knowledge. (The works of Robert Turner should be singled out for their insight and high level of scholarship.)

Some others I feel are of less value. While perhaps informative as examples of the "findings" of one magician's experimentation, the distinction is not always made clear as to what is the author's speculation and innovation and what actually are the procedures suggested in the original documents. Then, to make matters even more confusing, the author presumes to define to the reader what they can expect to experience, intimidating that if they get anything else they are somehow in error.

In my opinion, these works are little more than guided meditations upon another magician's visions and deny the reader the challenge of self discovery and mastery. But I'm sure that new volumes such as these will continue to appear. I will not be surprised to someday see titles such as *The Enochian Cookbook*, or *I'm OK...You're Enochian* appearing at my local bookstore.

It is our aim to offer in a practical format, *Liber LXXXIV vel Chanokh*, Crowley's original presentation of basic Enochiana and make it *immediately* useful for the student who wishes to make use of it *now*.

This coupled with Regardie's fine Enochian Dictionary and pronunciation guide provides the reader with the minimum material necessary to get started. For the advanced student we offer practical instructions concerning *powerful sexual applications* of the system and the opportunity to re-evaluate the original information that the greatest magician of the 20th Century felt was most necessary to master first.

Chapter One
A Short, Brief History (Abridged)

I have often read in thy [God's] books & records, how Enoch injoyed thy favour & conversation; with Moses thou was familiar; And also that to Abraham, Issack & Jacob, Joshua, Gideon, Esdras, Daniel, Tobias & sundry others thy good angels were sent by thy disposition, to Instruct them, informe them, helpe them, yea in worldly and domestick affaires, yea and sometymes to satisfie their desires, doubtes, and questions of thy Secrete.
Dr. John Dee (Sloane MS. 3188)

For God's sake, tell me what to think.   Asheigh Brilliant

It is said that the Enochian System of Magick, as practiced today, is the Child of Four Fathers; John Dee, Edward Kelly, S. L. MacGregor Mathers and Aleister Crowley. While this is a grossly inaccurate oversimplification (Dr. Rudd, Elias Ashmole, Wynn Westcott and Israel Regardie might at least be called midwives), it is basically true.

Through the efforts of the unbelievably mercurial Elizabethan mathematician, Dr. John Dee and his equally *unbelievable* "psychic" partner, Edward Kelly, the raw material for the Enochian System was "dictated" through a series of Angelic communications that lasted from 1582 to 1589. Copious records were kept, many of which have survived to the present.

Ironically, once Dee and Kelly went through the heroic effort to get all this information, it is believed they did not do a great deal with it. Miraculously, much of the material survived the nearly 3 centuries to come to the attention of S. L. Macgregor Mathers in the late 1880s.

(Note: Enochian fragments were even found in the famous cypher manuscripts whose discovery was instrumental in the creation of the Hermetic Order of the Golden Dawn.)

Mainly due to his inspired scholarship and impeccable logic, Dee's and Kelly's "raw" material was hammered into a comprehensive and workable system of ceremonial Magick. The two major branches of the system were then grafted to the Adeptus Minor curriculum of the Golden Dawn.

Aleister Crowley, who joined the Golden Dawn in 1898 and attained the Grade of Adeptus Minor in 1900, was of course exposed to the Order's Enochian teachings. However, Crowley took the Enochian "ball" and ran with it farther than the founders of the Golden Dawn had ever dreamed possible.

His exploration of the 30 Æthyrs as chronicled in *The Vision And The Voice (Gems From The Equinox,* Falcon Press, 1982) has been seriously compared to the visionary works of William Blake and the Qabalistic images of Ezekiel and the Revelation of Saint John the Divine.

It was also Aleister Crowley who reorganized and elucidated upon the Golden Dawn Enochian material and published it in *The Equinox Vol. I, Nos. VII and VIII* as *A Brief Abstract Of The Symbolic Representation Of The Universe Derived By Doctor John Dee Through The Skrying Of Sir Edward Kelly.* (Subsequently and mercifully renamed *Liber LXXXIV vel Chanokh.*)

CHAPTER TWO
Before We Start
Let's Get Something Straight

The student who waits to master the subject before proceeding to perform Magick, will never master the subject nor proceed to perform Magick or for that matter anything else.
Christopher S. Hyatt, Ph.D.

Anyone who refuses to begin a magical operation because of fear of "evil" forces that might be unleashed if he or she makes a mistake, has already made a mistake that has invoked a far greater "evil".
David P. Wilson

Resign yourself at the outset to take responsibility for your own magical reality. When you have firmly assumed this responsibility you will realize that there is no Enochian universe per se. There is only *your* universe which you can access by the Enochian formulae. There is no Enochian magick per se. There is only *your* magick, facilitated by the methods of the Enochian system.

This is not to argue the concept of spirits and angels having a certain objective reality. Indeed, the fundamental operating principle of evocation is to give outward substance to inner realities. But the sooner you rid yourself of preconceived ideas of how all this is going to manifest, the sooner you will be able to recognize it when it really *does* start to manifest.

For example, let us compare the Enochian system of Dr. Dee to a more familiar "system" of another Elizabethan genius.

The sensitive theater-goer reaps a rich harvest of intelletual and spiritual rewards whenever he or she sees a play by William Shakespeare.

Each character in the play, hero or villain, speaks the "truth" from their particular perspective and it is up to us, as the audience, to analyze these "truths" and apply them toward understanding our own lives.

Restated in Magickal Language: *Every Angel in the system, Divine or Demonic, declares their nature from their particular perspective and it is up to me, as the magician, to analyze their communication and apply that knowledge to the understanding of the Great Work.*

These "truths" would be the same "truths" if the actors were dressed traditionally, or as cowboys or as space aliens. Granted, *you* might be distracted and miss the point of Hamlet's soliloquy if it were delivered by a giant ameoba, but a Biologist might find it most profound.

Just as no two people see and react to a play in exactly the same way, so too, no two magicians will have identical experiences in evocation.

Dare To Be Lazy

If you are truly interested in peforming Enochian Magick, there is more than enough information between the covers of this book to help you grasp the theory, build the equipment and perform the magick. In fact, you are encouraged to do so.

By following the suggestions in the section that follows, you will avoid many time-consuming mistakes that have traditionally plagued the Enochian student.

Supplementary to the text of *Chanokh*, I have provided comments to each of the major sections and have additional diagrams in the Appendix. I strongly suggest that you read these and refer to the diagrams *while* you read *Chanokh*. You will save many hours of confusion and frustration if you will take this simple advice.

Also, pay special attention to the "Hints". They are put there to steer you clear of the "rocks" of Crowley's *thrifty* use of the English language (not to mention his downright omissions and a typo or two).

Make it easy on yourself. Dare to be lazy.

Chapter Three

The Ten Minute Overview

The two pillars of modern Enochian Magick, as outlined in *Liber Chanokh* (Chapter Five) are The Elemental Watch-Towers (including the Tablet of Union) and the "World" of the 30 Æthyrs. The first is:

**The Elemental Watch-Towers Of
The Universe And The Tablet Of Union**

These are the Elemental Tablets (Plates III, IV, V, VI, VII, and VIII) which are constructed with the purest Hermetic logic and lettered according to the diagrams of Dee and Kelly. These letters form the names of the Spirits of *Fire, Water, Air* and *Earth*.

These are the "Elementals" of literature: the Salamanders of Fire, the Undines of Water, the Sylphs of Air, and the Gnomes of Earth.

Exactly what are the Elements and, more importantly, why would anyone want to call up an Elemental Being? Below is a portion of the book *The Way of the Secret Lover: Tantra, Tarot and the Holy Guardian Angel* (New Falcon Publications, 1991) which touches upon the subject of the Elements.

> *The ancients viewed the Elements as the building blocks of creation. They divided them into four broad categories which they called FIRE, WATER, AIR and EARTH.*
>
> *Of course these are not the chemical elements which combine to form the material world around us. Nor are they literally Fire, Water, Air and Earth. They are, most simply put, the totality of all the forces, energies and qualities in the universe divided into four broad categories. These categories, by their nature, bear a resemblance to Fire, Water, Air and Earth. These qualities are the foundation of both galaxies and sub-atomic particles and the limitless diversity of creation is the result of the infinite number of ways these four Elements can be mixed, combined and recombined.*

It is interesting to note that modern physics postulates four fundamental forces; the **Strong Force,** *the* **Electro-Magnetic Force,** *the* **Weak Force** *and the* **Gravitational Force** *that, by their characteristics, bear a remarkable resemblance to the Ancient Elements.*

The ancients also postulated a Fifth Element (quite literally a "quintessence") which serves the double duty of binding the four Elements together and (at the same time) keeping them far enough apart to retain their individuality. This Fifth Element they called **SPIRIT.**

Once you have colored your Tablets you will see how the "Angels" of any given Element are formed, combined, mixed, recombined and reformed.

Obviously these Elementals are more than just the Salamanders in your fireplace, the sailor's Mermaid, Tinkerbell or Gimli the Dwarf. They have far more universal natures and as such are worthy of our attention. As a matter of fact, they are at work, either efficiently or inefficiently, in each of us. Perhaps if we had a better understanding of our Elemental balance (or lack of it) we might get a clue as to how to improve our lives.

Note: What follows may seem a bit complicated to the new student. A full explanation of the operating procedure will be given in the following chapters.

For example, some years ago I accepted a job from an old friend who asked me to edit a psychology book he had just completed. I had never done such a thing before and I accepted with some hesitation.

The evening before I was to start, I decided to invoke an Enochian Elemental Angel to help me put things in perspective and perhaps to give me a little boost on my first day. I chose to invoke **SOAIZNT** the Mercury Senior of the *Water* Tablet. (My reasoning was that Mercury is the force that is traditionally associated with writing and matters of the mind, and Water is the element of reflection and empathy which I felt would be necessary for a task such as this.)

The invocation was simple enough. I had my Tablet of Union and Elemental Tablets sitting upon a table in the center of the room. After a routine Banishing Ritual of the Pentagram, I opened the

Temple in the Grade of 3°=8 as written in *Chanokh*, then performed the Hexagram Ritual invoking Mercury (Planetary Seniors are invoked by the Hexagram), then I simply recited the *Fourth Call* straight out of *Chanokh*.

At first I "saw" nothing. (My skrying technique is to sit quietly with my eyes closed.) I felt somewhat stimulated and remember thinking that I should do this ritual whenever I needed to stay awake—when suddenly *it* was there. It had a basic humanoid form but it looked as if it had a "skin" made entirely of silver reflective material. Not stiff like a series of mirrors or facets, but smooth, almost liquid. Everywhere I looked on its "body" I saw myself reflected. It was breathtakingly beautiful. I was dumbfounded. After a moment when I could think straight again, I repeated the name, **SOAIZNT** (the standard procedure to test a vision). It seemed to gain strength and become clearer with each repetition of its name so I felt confident that what was in front of me was indeed what I had called up. The question was now 'what am I going to do with this guy'? It took a little effort but I finally remembered the reason for the operation. I asked if it could help me to better understand another's thoughts and to efficiently transfer these thoughts to the written word. It indicated it could and produced a mirror upon which it drew a figure. I "felt" that I was to somehow use this figure as a tool to achieve my goal. I drew it on a piece of scratch paper and after the obligatory banishing I gazed upon it for a few minutes then went to bed. The next morning I decided I would take the figure **SOAIZNT** gave me and simply draw it at the top of each page of my daily note pad where I would be forced to look at it almost continually. Throughout the course of the project (which went surprisingly well by the way), I was focused upon this symbol and constantly reminded of the invocation and the incredible vision of the Angel who aids works of this nature.

In practical workings such as this it is very helpful to bring s*omething* from the vision back into *this* world.

In the *everyday* world of our waking consciousness, life forms such as people, animals, plants, etc., we perceive as living "beings." On the other hand, symbols such as triangles, pentagrams, letters, etc., we perceive as abstractions, springboards to a variety of ideas. In the "magical" world it is just the opposite. When we "see" a life form, such as an Angel or a unicorn or an aardvark, it is an abstract personification of an idea. Symbols, on the other hand, are "living beings" on that plane, the true life forms of the magical universe.

As you can imagine these symbol-life forms can be powerful tools in the hands of the magician. Bringing them through to our objective world is an important part of practical workings.

The second pillar is:

**The Thirty Æthyrs Whose Dominion
Extendeth In Ever-Widening Circles Beyond
The Watch-Towers Of The Universe**

These are the "heavens" or Aires of the system. Starting with the *30th Æthyr* and the working of the *1st*, the magician explores only as far as his or her personal level of Initiation will permit. This process is comparable to "pathworkings" of the Qabalistic system. In Enochian terms, the "Great Work" of the magician is to master all 30 Æthyrs. (Starting with 30 and ending with 1.)

Experiences with the 30 Æthyrs are highly personal and entirely unique to each magician. Working with the Æthyrs can be a lifetime endeavor and it is entirely presumptuous and inappropriate for another individual to "guide" another in this area.

Thus, with these two branches of the system, the Elemental and the Æthyric, we have formulae to access both the phenomenal world of the Elements and the private world of our own Spiritual Journey.

Both types of operations require the ability on the part of the magician to skry or "travel in the Spirit Vision." If you are not already a talented skryer, there is no better way to train than Enochian Magick, especially elemental workings.

There are as many skrying techniques as there are magicians who skry. Dee and Kelly gazed into a concave obsidian mirror. Crowley held a large topaz mounted upon a wooden cross to his forehead. But other methods include gazing into crystals, ink, fire or even a blank TV screen. You can sit in a chair or on the floor or lie on your back. You can close your eyes or keep them open. Use what works for you. As it is a subjective (well, maybe not entirely subjective) experience, the choice is yours. I was amused to hear one skryer's abilities criticized for being done in a "light trance" state. We should be so lucky!

For anyone who has tried unsuccessfully to skry in the past, I offer the following hint.

Stop trying to skry!

Don't try to "see" a vision in your mind. The vision is already going on in the part of your mind (the right side of the brain) where you are not currently focused. (Don't criticize the movie if you go to the theater, buy a ticket then choose to stay in the lobby.) When you refocus your attention to that part of your mind you will find the "vision" in progress. It's impossible to refocus while you are consciously *trying* to refocus. So stop *trying*. Relax.

This change of focus happens each time you drop off to sleep. There is a moment when your thoughts begin to take visual form. You have a choice for a brief moment of "snapping out of it" or relaxing and "going with it," allowing yourself to change your focus for the rest of the night.

When you skry you are not asleep but neither are you focused on the objective world as analyzed by the left side of your brain. You relax and *allow* yourself to focus on the subjective, visual world of your brain's right hemisphere.

The most important thing to remember is not to project an objective reality to another skryer's vision This is the flaw of "guided Pathworkings" or meditations upon another magician's visions. It is *your* magical universe you are dealing with and no one else's. (You are well advised to test your own visions and take them with a rather large grain of salt as well.)

Chapter Four

Comments on Liber LXXXIV vel Chanokh

THE TITLE "LIBER LXXXIV"
The original title first published in *The Equinox* Vol. 1, Nos. VII and VIII was *A Brief Abstract Of The Symbolic Representation Of The Universe Derived By Dr. John Dee Through The Skrying Of Sir Edward Kelly*.

LXXXIV (84) is the Qabalistic numeratin for *Chanokh*, the Hebrew spelling of Enoch.

Note: When originally published the title did not bear the number. Crowley assigned the number 84 when the Syllabus of the Official Instructions of A∴A∴ was published in *The Blue Equinox*. Since then, due to a series of typographical errors, the number *LXXXIX* (89) has been mistakenly used in the title of published works. For our purposes I will refer to it simply as *Chanokh*.

PART I
THE HOLY TWELVEFOLD TABLE

The Holy Table is part of the "furniture" of the Temple and does not directly concern Elemental or Æthyrical workings. Angels found on the Holy Table are not called forth in these operations.

The original table top measured $35^{7}/_{8}$ in x $36^{1}/_{4}$ in x $^{7}/_{10}$ in.

Note: There is good reason to believe that the illustration as printed in *Chanokh* (Plate I) is in error. Plate I is reproduced from Casaubon's *A True and Faithful Relation of What Passed for Many Years Between Dr. John Dee and Some Spirits*...published in 1659. It is now believed that, due to a 17th Century printer's error, Casaubon's version (and consequently everybody's since) was printed with the letters in reverse order. One of Dee's descriptions of the Table indicates it resembled the illustration I have included in Appendix I (Diagram A) of this book. This is regarded as the correct version. (Note: The Plates referred to are *not* in the Appendix but in the text of *Chanokh* itself [Chapter Five of this book]. All of the diagrams are in the Appendix of this book and are not original *Chanokh* illustrations.)

THE SEVEN TALISMANS

Like the Holy Table, these are considered Temple "furniture" and do not directly concern Elemental or Æthyrical workings. Spirits found on these talismans are not called forth in these operations.

The illustrations in Plate I are too small to read. Enlargements from the 17th Century manuscript, Dr. Rudd's Treatise, are included in Appendix I (Diagram B) of this book. It is interesting to note that the names on these "planetary" talismans are those of the Goetia. This indicates (or at least implies) Dee's familiarity with the LEMEGETON and his attempt, at least early in his workings, to incorporate it in the Enochian system.

PART II
THE HOLY SEVENFOLD TABLE:
THE SIGILLUM DEI ÆMETH

Perhaps the most widely recognized diagram of the Enochian system, the *Sigillum Dei Æmeth* does not directly concern Elemental or Æthyrical workings. Like the Holy Table and Talismans, its Angels are not called forth in these operations. Nevertheless it is an important piece of temple "furniture," for upon it rested the Shew-stone or the skrying mirror.

Made from bee's wax as described in Chanokh, the four smaller versions were placed under the feet of the Holy Table, presumably to insulate it from "earthy vibrations". The fifth and larger one (about 9 inches in diameter) covered with a red cloth, was placed on the Holy Table to support the Shew-stone.

Note: The illustration on Plate II was taken from Dee's diaries. The large wax version on display at the British Museum is slightly different. For example, on the actual wax version there are 7 crosses on each of the 7 bars making up the main heptagram. The illustration shows only three bars with 7 crosses, the other 4 containing only 3.

Even though the above items of temple furniture are unnecessary for Elemental operations and for exploring the 30 Æthyrs, the reader might like to make his or her own versions of them to support the skrying mirror. Many of my (dare to be lazy) students have simply made photographic enlargements of the illustrations that appear in this book and have mounted them on wood or foam board.

PART III

This is the most important section for the student to grasp. It deals directly with the two branches of the system of the most practical value, *The Elemental Tablets and the Tablet of Union* (sometimes referred to as the Black Cross) and the *30 Æthyrs* or Aires. By using the information in this section the serious student will eventually construct the fabled equipment of the art.

This is also where many become confused and discouraged. Admittedly it will take the reader's full attention to wade through this section. This is not because Crowley is being deliberately obscure. On the contrary, it is because he is being almost unbelievably economical with his choice of words and the ordering of his thoughts.

I hope the following hints will save you some difficult moments.

HINT #1 BE PREPARED FOR INCONSISTENCES IN THE LETTERING OF THE TABLETS

Don't panic when you discover alternate spellings to names drawn from the Elemental Tablets. This is due to the fact that Dee and Kelly (at the direction of the communicating angels) made several revisions to the tablets. To help you, we have included in Appendix I charts showing alternate and multiple lettering (See Diagram E).

HINT #2 CAREFULLY READ AND REFER OFTEN TO THE PLATES

A picture is worth a thousand words and in this case many hours. To be able to see what Crowley is writing about will save you much valuable time. Plates IV, V, VI, VII and VIII are lettered in Enochian. For English equivalents refer to Appendix I (assorted diagrams).

> HINT #3
> REMEMBER, THE SAME GENERAL LAWS APPLY TO ALL FOUR ELEMENTAL TABLETS. TO UNDERSTAND ONE IS TO UNDERSTAND THEM ALL

For example; Crowley explains the Hierarchy of the *Three Holy Names*, the *Great Elemental King*, the *Six Seniors*, the *Two Divine Names of the Calvary Cross*, the *Kerubim* and the *Sixteen Lesser Angels* by using the Water Tablet (Plate V) as the example. The Hierarchy of the Fire, Air, and Earth Tablets are determined in exactly the same way.

Note: To make this section easier to understand, I have included in Appendix I (Diagram D) an English version of the *Water Tablet* conveniently split apart for easy viewing. If you keep this diagram in front of you while reading Part III of *Chanokh,* I think you will have no trouble understanding what is being said.

BASIC TERMS

The Four Great Watch-Towers are often referred to as the Elemental Tablets of Air, Water, Earth and Fire.

Plate III shows them together: *Air* in the upper left-hand quarter, *Water* in the upper right-hand quarter, *Earth* in the lower left-hand quarter and *Fire* in the lower right-hand quarter.

Plates IV, V, VI and VII show them singularly. Each of the Elemental Tablets is also divided into four sections by the two central vertical columns and the central horizontal line (the *Linea Patris*, the *Linea Filii* and the *Linea Spiritus Sancti* respectively). This is also referred to as the Great Central Cross of the Elemental Tablet. (See Diagram D.)

The four sections of the Elemental Tablet created by the Great Central Cross are called Subangles which are also attributed to the four Elements (*Air* in the upper left-hand quarter, *Water* in the upper right-hand quarter, *Earth* in the lower left-hand quarter, and *Fire* in the lower right-hand quarter).

In Diagram D of Appendix I of this book, you will see an example of the Water Table divided by the Great Central Cross and broken into its Subangles (*Air of Water* in the upper-left, *Water of Water* in the upper-right, *Earth of Water* in the lower-left, and *Fire of Water* in the lower-right). Subangles on the *Air*, *Fire* and *Earth* Tablets are arranged in *exactly the same way*.

1. THE THREE HOLY NAMES OF GOD

(See Diagram D.) The Three Holy Names of God are made up of the first three letters, the next four letters and the last five letters of the *Linea Spiritus Santci* (the central horizontal line of each Elemental Tablet). For our example, the *Water* Tablet, the Three Holy Names are: **MPH ARSL GAIOL**.

Note: Don't let these names intimidate you. Just locate them. Don't worry about pronouncing them now. There is an excellent pronunciation guide provided later in this book.

Now try to locate The Three Holy Names on the Fire, Air and Earth Tablets.

2. THE GREAT ELEMENTAL KING

(See Diagram D.) The eight letter Name of the Great Elemental King is formed by a clockwise whorl around the center of The Great Central Cross of the *Linea Patris*, the *Linea Filii* and the *Linea Spiritus Sancti*. The Great Elemental King may be considered the Sun Senior of the Tablet. The Great Elemental King of the *Water* Tablet is **RAAGIOSL**. Now try to locate the Great Elemental Kings on the other three Elemental Tablets.

3. THE SIX SENIORS

(See Diagram D.) The 7 letter Names of the Six Planetary Seniors are also drawn from the Great Central Cross. Each Name starts in the middle of the Cross and moves towards the extremities. (Arrows in Diagram D show the directions the names are read and the Planet to which each of the Seniors is attributed.) **This is the same for all four Elemental Tablets.**

In the case of the *Water* Tablet; **SAIINOV** is the Senior of Jupiter, **SOAIZNT** is the Senior of Mercury, **LAOAZRP** is the Senior of the Moon, **LIGDISA** is the Senior of Saturn, **SLGAIOL** is the Senior of Venus and **LSRAHPM** is the Senior of Mars. Now locate the Six Seniors on the three other Elemental Tablets.

4. THE CALVARY CROSSES

(See Diagram D.) Each of the four Subangles on an Elemental Tablet contains a Calvary Cross. The two Angels of the Calvary Cross rule the Subangle. With the first Name (the vertical line—reading from top to bottom) you call forth the Power of the Subangle. With the second Name (the horizontal line—reading from left to right) you compel the Power to obedience. (We will see how to do this later.) These names as they apply to the *Water* Tablet appear in the text of *Chanokh*.

Remember, there are four Calvary Crosses in each Elemental Tablet. Now locate the four Calvary Crosses in the subangles of each of the four Elemental Tablets.

5. KERUBIM

(See Diagram D.) The four letter Name of the Kerub is found above the arms of the Calvary Cross of each subangle. The letters of the Cross itself are never included in the Kerub's name.

The Kerub rules the *angels* who reside below the arms of the Cross. The four letters in the name of the Kerub can be rearranged in different orders to create different Kerubs who in turn rule different *angels* beneath the arms of the cross. (The letters of their names rearranged exactly as those of the rearranged Kerub.)

Note: A great deal of confusion exists concerning this statement in *Chanokh*.

They are ruled by names of God formed by prefixing the appropriate letter from the 'black cross' to their own [the Kerubim] names…There is disagreement among scholars as to which letters from the "Black Cross" (the Tablet of Union) are "appropriate." If you refer to Diagram G you will see that 16 of the 20 squares correspond to the 16 subangles of the four Elemental tablets.

The most popular theory maintains that these are the appropriate letters to help form the name of the "God" that rules the Kerub of any given Subangle. Let us use the example of the Elemental Tablet of *Water* (Diagram D). The Kerub of the Subangle of *Fire* is **NLRX**. Now refer to Diagram G and find the *Fire of Water* square. It is the fifth square of the second line. "**A**" (the "**A**" in **HCOMA**). So the God that rules **NLRX** would be **ANLRX**.

Please remember that there is disagreement, even among very knowledgeable experts, about these "God" names and where exactly they fit in the Enochian Hierarchy.

I advise beginning students to first become adequately fluent in basic hierarchical workings, then develop for themselves a structure for those "supercharged" angels. The system does not pivot on this point.

6. THE FOUR MIGHTY AND BENEVOLENT ANGELS

(See Diagram D.) These **Angels** are found beneath the horizontal bar of the Calvary Cross and are last in the Hierarchy of the Elemental Angels. They are extremely interesting and can provide great insight into the nature of the Elements. (Again, the names are only of four letters.)

Note: Remember these four Angels are ruled by their Kerub who is found above the horizontal arm of the Calvary Cross. When you make a different Kerub (by changing the order of the letters in its name) you automatically make four new sets of Angel names beneath the arm of the Calvary Cross (by changing the order of the letters of their names in the same manner as the new Kerub).

7. THE DEMONS OR ELEMENTALS

(See Diagram D.) Unfortunately the definitive instructions promised by Crowley were not forthcoming, and experts and students alike are left to speculate and disagree. The reader is encouraged to join in this quest. It is clear that they are not routinely called forth in workings of the Elemental Tablets.

[Following Crowley's comments on the Triliteral names of demons (above) he begins a second section of PART III with subheadings 1-5.]

PART III
(SECOND SECTION)

As you can see from Plates IV, V, VI, VII and VIII, the Squares of the Elemental Tablets and the Tablet of Union are really Pyramids with flat tops. The Pyramid with its four sides and top is an especially appropriate symbol for the Four Elements ruled by Spirit. Each side of an Enochian Pyramid has a very specific attribute.

There are 20 Pyramids in the Tablet of Union and 156 in each of the four Elemental tablets. Each Pyramid houses an Angel with a one letter name. The attributes of that Angel are determined by the positioning of the Pyramid upon the Tablet and proportions of the different Elements represented on its four sides. When two Pyramids are combined they form an Angel with a two letter name whose attributes are a bit more complex. And so on.

To easily understand how these attributes are determined, I will give the reader *the most valuable hint of all*:

HINT #4
HAND COLOR PLATES
IV, V, VI, VII and VIII

Before attempting to understand the second section of Part III, you are well advised to make photocopies of Plates IV, V, VI, VII and VIII and then hand color the Pyramids. By coloring the Pyramids you will learn, in the fastest and easiest way possible, the logic behind their construction.

THE COLORING KEY FOR EACH PYRAMID

Leave the center square of each Pyramid (which contains the letter) uncolored for the time being.

Sides with the *Spirit* Symbol	✵	White
Sides with the *Fire* Symbol	△	Red
Sides with the *Water* Symbol	▽	Blue
Sides with the *Air* Symbol	𝐀	Yellow
Sides with the *Earth* Symbol	⍌	Green or Black

I suggest you start with the Tablet of Union (Plate VIII or the English lettered version in Appendix I, Diagram G). Even though it is small, it is a very important Tablet for its Angels, **EXARP, HCOMA, NANTA** and **BITOM**, rule the other four Elemental Tablets. (**EXARP** rules the *Air* Tablet, **HCOMA** rules the *Water* Tablet, **NANTA** rules the *Earth* Tablet and **BITOM** rules the *Fire* Tablet.)

The Tablet Of Union is considered the Elemental Tablet of *Spirit*. The four Elements are represented in their purest form, undifferentiated by the level of admixture that characterizes the other four Elements. It binds them together so they can combine to be the building blocks of creation *yet* keeps them separated just enough to prevent the loss of their individual and fundamental natures. This active and passive quality of Spirit is the reason that there are *two* types of Spirit Pentagrams, Active and Passive.

The Angels of the Tablet of Union can be said to be the very "roots" of the Angels of the Elemental Tablets.

Once you have colored your Tablet of Union, you will discover that a very simple pattern is formed by the attributes in the *Lines* and *Files* (or *Columns*). The top and bottom section of each Pyramid is attributed to Spirit. The right side is attributed to the Primary Element (as dictated by which *Line* the Pyramid is located) and the left side is attributed to the Secondary Element (as dictated by which *Column* it is located).

Note: This and what follows below will be laughably easy to understand if you have taken *five minutes* and colored your Tablet of Union.

THE LINES

The four five letter Names (**EXARP, HCOMA, NANTA** and **BITOM**) are the Primary Spirits of the Elements. Each Spirit governs an entire Elemental Tablet.

EXARP is the Spirit of Air and governs the entire Air Tablet. The right section of each Pyramid of **EXARP** is Air.

HCOMA is the Spirit of Water and governs the entire Water Tablet. The right section of each Pyramid of **HCOMA** is Water.

NANTA is the Spirit of Earth and governs the entire Earth

Tablet. The right section of each Pyramid of **NANTA** is Earth.
BITOM is the Spirit of Fire and governs the entire Fire Tablet. The right section of each Pyramid of **BITOM** is Fire.

THE COLUMNS

The same order of Air, Water, Earth and Fire is repeated in the Columns of the Tablet of Union as Secondary attributions which appear on the left section of the Pyramid. (See Diagram G.)

The first Column, **EHNB** is the purest of all the Column Names.

Each letter rules its respective Line and is three parts Spirit and one part its respective Element.

    E governs **EXARP**
    H governs **HCOMA**
    N governs **NANTA**
    B governs **BITOM.**

The sixteen letters of the remaining four column contain both Primary and Secondary attributions. (Remember, the Secondary attribution is located upon the left section of these Pyramids.) These sixteen letters govern the sixteen Subangles of the Elemental Tablets.

    X = Air of Air   **A** = Water of Air
    C = Air of Water   **O** = Water of Water
    A = Air of Earth   **N** = Water of Earth
    I = Air of Fire   **T** = Water of Fire
    R = Earth of Air   **P** = Fire of Air
    M = Earth of Water **A** = Fire of Water
    T = Earth of Earth **A** = Fire of Earth
    O = Earth of Fire   **M** = Fire of Fire

An easy way to think about how the Tablet of Union relates to the other four Tablets is to pretend you have an "Elemental Microscope."

Take the letter **E** from **EXARP** and put it under your microscope. You will see the entire *Air* Elemental Tablet.

Take the letter **O** from **BITOM** and put it under your microscope. You will see the *Earth* Subangle of the Tablet of *Fire*.

Take the second letter **N** from **NANTA** and put it under your microscope. You will see the *Water* Subangle of the *Earth* Tablet, etc.

After you have colored your Tablet of Union, color each of the four Elemental Tablets.

HINT #5
COLOR EACH ELEMENTAL TABLET IN FOUR STEPS

Note: There are various ways the Pyramids of the Great Central Cross may be colored. We have chosen the method below because the attributes are uniformly determined through Elemental rulerships.

STEP 1:
THE GREAT CENTRAL CROSS

The **Top** section of each Pyramid of the **Great Central Cross** represents **Spirit** and is painted White.

The *Bottom* section of each Pyramid of the Great Central Cross represents the Element of the Tablet. In the case of the *Water* Tablet it is painted Blue. (When painting the *Fire* Tablet the bottom sections of the Great Central Cross would be Red, the *Air* Tablet Yellow, the *Earth* Tablet, Green or Black).

The *Left* side of each Pyramid of the Great Central Cross represents the Signs of the Zodiac. These are grouped in threes by element and positioned as described in *Chanokh*.

The *Fire* Signs (Aires, Leo and Sagittarius) are colored Red.

The *Water* Signs (Cancer, Scorpio and Pisces) are colored Blue.

The *Air* Signs (Libra, Aquarius and Gemini) are colored Yellow.

The *Earth* Signs (Capricorn, Taurus and Virgo) are colored Green (or Black).

The *Right* side of each Pyramid of the Great Central Cross represents the planetary rulership of the 36 decans of the Zodiac. There are 36 decans and 36 Pyramids in the Great Central Cross. For our purpose we color the planets according to the rulership of the fixed signs:

Saturn and Mercury for *Air* are colored Yellow.

Jupiter and the Sun for *Fire* are colored Red.

Venus and the Moon for *Earth* are colored Green or (Black).

Mars for *Water* is colored Blue.

STEP 2:
THE CALVARY CROSSES

The *Top* section of each Pyramid of the Calvery Crosses of the subangles represents *Spirit* and is painted white.

The *Bottom* section of the Pyramid of the Calvary Crosses of the subangles represents one of the ten *Sephiroth* of the Qabalistic Tree of Life and the sections are numbered according to Plates IV, V, VI and VII. We suggest, for the time being, that you leave the Bottom sections White and simply number them in Black. Later you may wish to paint them one of the four traditional colors of the Sephiroth.

The *Left* section of each Pyramid of the Calvary Crosses of the subangles represents the Element of the Tablet. In the case of *Water* Tablet, the Left section of the Pyramids of each of the four Calvary Crosses will be painted Blue.

The *Right* section of each Pyramid of the Calvary Crosses of the subangles represents the Element of the subangle itself and is painted accordingly. [Upper Left-hand subangle (Air – Yellow), Upper Right-hand subangle (Water – Blue), Lower Left-hand subangle (Earth – Green or Black), Lower Right-hand subangle (Fire – Red)]. This pattern is the same for all four Elemental Tablets.

STEP 3:
THE KERUBIC ANGELS

These are found above the arms of the Calvary Crosses.

The *Top* section of each of the four Kerubic Pyramids represents the Elemental Tablet and is colored accordingly. In the case of the Water Tablet, Blue.

The *Bottom* section of each of the four Kerubic Pyramids represents the Element of the subangle itself and is colored accordingly.

Color the *Right* and *Left* sections of each of the four Kerubic Pyramids as indicated in Plates IV, V, VI and VII. The order that the elements are arranged follow a logical permutation and dictate the order of the Lines and Columns of the 16 Lesser Pyramids found below the arms of the Calvary Cross.

STEP 4:
THE 16 LESSER PYRAMIDS

These are found below the arms of the Calvary Crosses.

The *Left* section of each Pyramid of the Lesser Angels represents the Elemental Tablet. In the case of the *Water* Tablet it is colored Blue.

The *Right* section of each Pyramid of the Lesser Angels represents the subangle and is colored accordingly.

Color the *Top* and *Bottom* section of each of the sixteen Lesser Pyramids as indicated in Plates IV, V, VI and VII. Notice how the coloring order is dictated by the squares of the Kerubic Angels.

Granted, all this may take a few hours to execute but it will save you months (or as in my case, years) of confusion.

Now with your colored Tablets before you, read the material in the Second section of Part III of *Chanokh* and marvel at the "method" to the "madness."

PART IV
THE ENOCHIAN ALPHABET
AND THE ENOCHIAN LANGUAGE

One of the most unique characteristics of Enochian Magick is that the invocations are recited in a language completely unique to the system.

This language comes down to us as the result of the workings of Dr. John Dee and Edward Kelly and, according to their records, was taught to them by the Enochian Angels themselves.

Israel Regardie in his massive work, *The Complete Golden Dawn System of Magic* (New Falcon Publications, 1984), makes the following comments:

> *The Enochian language is without any history prior to the skrying of Edward Kelly and John Dee. There is no record of its prior existence, regardless of some fanciful theories which have been invented to account for it. The Enochian language is not just a haphazard combination and compilation of divine and angelic names drawn form the Tablets. Apparently, it is a true language with a grammar and syntax of its own. Only a superficial study of the invocations suffice to indicate this to be a fact. The invocations are not strings of words and barbarous names, but are sentences which can be translated in a meaningful way and not merely transliterated.*

I believe, when invoking, that it is of the utmost importance to recite the Call or Calls in Enochian and not use an English translation. Not that it is unimportant for the Magician to know exactly what is being said but it is obvious to me that the intelligences who delivered this language to Dee and Kelly did not do it to hear themselves talk.

Reciting in Enochian instantly changes one's consciousness and induces a state of mind conducive to magical working.

The Calls themselves are very unique and are nothing like the tedious beseechments and endless whining of self debasement that characterize Goetic evocations. Rather, in the Angel's native tongue, they *sing* of its attributes and environment, and offer a dignified invitation to communicate with the Magician.

This format is irresistible to the Angel. Think about it. If a mouse crawled up on your shoe and started to squeak, you would only give it as much attention as you would need to chase it away. But if it crawled up on your shoe, called you by name and then began to recite, in English, a litany of recognizable personal traits:

...Oh thou who art so huge, who wakest with the music of the clockradio and who bringest in the morning paper, who with thy mouth consumest the eggs of the hen and wipeth thy lips with paper...

...you would sit up and take notice. You might even try to have a meaninful conversation with the little fellow. You wouldn't even mind if he spoke with a thick accent!

The Enochian Calls as they appear in *Chanokh* are written phonetically and are very close to the standard ones used by the Golden Dawn which appear in Regardie's Enochian Dictionary in Appendix III of this book.

Plate IX shows the Enochian Alphabet and Plates I, IV, V, VII, VIII are lettered in Enochian.

PART V
THE THIRTY ÆTHYRS OR AIRES

As we will read in *Chanokh*, Crowley says that Dee:

...symbolized the Fourth-Dimensional Universe in two dimensions as a square surrounded by 30 concentric circles (the 30 Æthyrs or Aires) whose radii increase in a geometrical proportion.

The "square" mentioned in the previous paragraph is the Four Elemental Tablets and the Tablet of Union. These are quite literally Watch-Towers that stand at the very edge of the phenomenal universe. Beyond the Watch-Towers are the Æthyrs, the Aires, the Heavens. They can be visualized as thirty spheres, one inside another like layers of a glass onion. The Thirtieth, **TEX,** is the lowest and consequently the closest to the Watch-Towers.

LIL, the First, is the highest and represents the Supreme Attainment. It is the Great Work of the Magician to "explore" the Æthyrs one at a time, and learn the lessons, master the problems and receive the wisdom each has to offer.

Most anyone who cares to try has some level of success in the lower Æthyrs. It is important to keep a detailed record of all workings because eventually you will reach a point beyond which you cannot pass. This point marks the limits of your present level of "initiation" and the last Æthyr you *could* successfully penetrate holds the key to your spiritual advancement.

Each of the Thirty Æthyrs is populated by Governors whose responsibilities are partially described in Dee's *Liber Scientiæ, Auxilii, et Victoriæ Terrestris*. For our purpose, we will view the Governors as angelic personifications of the different facets of the Æthyrs. They serve as our guides and most importantly they are "someone" to whom we can talk and ask questions. The names of each of the Thrity Æthyrs and their Governors is provided in the text of *Chanokh*.

Each Æthyr has three Governors (except the Thirtieth which has four). Sigils (signatures) of the Governors are taken from the Elemental Tablets showing that the influence of the Æthyrs is universal, reaching even into the Watch-Towers of the Elements.

These sigils of the Governors are illustrated in Plate X and more clearly in Diagram F in Appendix I and are numbered 1 through 91. In order to more easily find the Sigil of each Governor, the reader is encouraged to number the list of Governors as found in Part V of *Chanokh* starting with **OCCODON-1, PASCOMB-2, VALGARS-3, DOAGNIS-4**, etc.

Ironically, very little effort is required to "work" with the Æthyrs. One Call only is necessary for all thirty of them. The name of the Æthyr itself being the only variable.

Once the Call is recited the names of the Governors are vibrated one at a time. Often the vision changes drastically when the next Governor's name is vibrated. Take your time with each one and, as always, keep a detailed record of your operation.

Now let us turn our attention to the section of *Chanokh* designated in the text as:

PART II
THE FORTY-EIGHT CALLS OR KEYS

The Calls or Keys activate the tablets and subangles in the same way as the power switch turns on a TV before selecting a channel.

At the beginning of this section, Crowley tells us which Calls are used in all the various invocations of the Elemental system. He does so in the fewest words humanly possible. Perhaps the reader will appreciate the elucidation below.

FIRST KEY

Use first in all invocations of any of the Angels of the Tablet of Union. (It is not used in the invocation of any of the Angels of the Elemental Tablets.)

SECOND KEY

Use second as invocation of the Angels of the letters **E H N B** of the Tablet of Union. Like the FIRST CALL, it is never used in the invocation of the Angels of the four Elemental Tablets. (The sequence of Calls being 1 and 2.)

Note: The Third, Fourth, Fifth and Sixth Keys are used in certain invocations of the Tablet of Union *and* in the Invocations of the Elemental Tablets. What follows immediately is how they are used in invocations of the Tablet of Union.

THIRD KEY

For invocations of the Angels of the letters of the line **EXARP**, the sequence of the Calls is 1, 2 and 3.

FOURTH KEY

For invocations of the Angels of the letters of the line **HCOMA**, the sequence of the Calls is 1, 2 and 4.

FIFTH KEY

For invocations of the Angels of the letters of the line **NANTA**, the sequence of the Calls is 1, 2 and 5.

SIXTH KEY

For invocations of the Angels of the letters of the line **BITOM**, the sequence of the Calls is 1, 2 and 6.

THE ELEMENTAL TABLETS
THIRD KEY AIR

Use first in all invocations of the Angels of the Tablet of Air. (When invoking a Senior or the Angels of subangle Air of Air it is the only call necessary.)

FOURTH KEY WATER

Use first in all invocations of the Angels of the Tablet of Water. (When invoking a Senior or the Angels of subangle Water of Water it is the only call necessary.)

FIFTH KEY EARTH

Use first in all invocations of the Angels of the Tablet of Earth. (When invoking a Senior or the Angels of subangle Earth of Earth it is the only call necessary.)

SIXTH KEY FIRE

Use first in all invocations of the Angels of the Tablet of Fire. (When invoking a Senior or the Angels of subangle Fire of Fire it is the only call necessary.)

SEVENTH KEY
WATER SUBANGLE OF AIR TABLET

For invocations of the Angels of the Water subangle of the Air Tablet, the sequence of Calls is 3 and 7.

EIGHTH KEY
EARTH SUBANGLE OF AIR TABLET

For invocations of the Angels of the Earth subangle of the Air Tablet, the sequence of Calls is 3 and 8.

NINTH KEY
FIRE SUBANGLE OF AIR TABLET

For invocations of the Angels of the Fire subangle of the Air Tablet, the sequence of Calls is 3 and 9.

TENTH KEY
AIR SUBANGLE OF WATER TABLET

For invocations of the Angels of the Air subangle of the Water Tablet, the sequence of Calls is 4 and 10.

ELEVENTH KEY
EARTH SUBANGLE OF WATER TABLET
For invocations of the Angels of the Earth subangle of the Water Tablet, the sequence of Calls is 4 and 11.

TWELFTH KEY
FIRE SUBANGLE OF WATER TABLET
For invocations of the Angels of the Fire subangle of the Water Tablet, the sequence of Calls is 4 and 12.

THIRTEENTH KEY
AIR SUBANGLE OF EARTH TABLET
For invocations of the Angels of the Air subangle of the Earth Tablet, the sequence of Calls is 5 and 13.

FOURTEENTH KEY
WATER SUBANGLE OF EARTH TABLET
For invocations of the Angels of the Water subangle of the Earth Tablet, the sequence of Calls is 5 and 14.

FIFTEENTH KEY
FIRE SUBANGLE OF EARTH TABLET
For invocations of the Angels of the Fire subangle of the Earth Tablet, the sequence of Calls is 5 and 15.

SIXTEENTH KEY
AIR SUBANGLE OF FIRE TABLET
For invocations of the Angels of the Air subangle of the Fire Tablet, the sequence of Calls is 6 and 16.

SEVENTEENTH KEY
WATER SUBANGLE OF FIRE TABLET
For invocations of the Angels of the Water subangle of the Fire Tablet, the sequence of Calls is 6 and 17.

EIGHTEENTH KEY
EARTH SUBANGLE OF FIRE TABLET
For invocations of the Angels of the Earth subangle of the Fire Tablet, the sequence of Calls is 6 and 18.

THE CALL OR KEY
OF THE THIRTY ÆTHYRS

As we have mentioned above, the Nineteenth Call, or Key of the Thirty Æthyrs, is the only call necessary for workings with the Æthyrs. It is only necessary to change the name of the Æthyr itself near the beginning of the Call.

Note: In a footnote in *Chanokh*, Crowley mentions a second name in the Call that *"...may appropriately be varied with the Aire"*. Try as I may to discover a logical correlation between **LIL** (the Æthyr in question) and **IDOIGO** (the footnoted name in question), I cannot. Until I do, I will continue to vary the Call of the Thirty Æthyrs only with the name of the Æthyr itself. If I am wrong, I am willing to be forgiven.

MINIMUM RECOMMENDED
OPERATING PROCEDURES

The question now arises, "How do I go about implementing the above information to invoke the Angels of the Elemental Tablets or begin my exploration of the Æthyrs?"

The nature of the original Dee material is such as to make exact and definitive operating procedures unclear. In other books of Enochian Magick, particularly those written in the last 10 years, you will find elaborate instructions that differ considerably from what is suggested below.

As you become more familiar with the system you will develop your own sense of what is logical and appropriate. It is very important during the period of your learning curve to stay focused on source material such as *Chanokh*.

Chanokh provides basic operating instructions, though not always clearly. It is obvious that Crowley assumed readers would have a basic magical education and would be able to proceed somewhat on their own understanding. These comments and the supplementary material in the Appendices are intended to help on both these fronts. But we should not ignore the obvious fact that Crowley's original presentation was very short and straightforward. Nowhere does he even hint that the Magician must engage in a long series of beseechments, coercions and just plain magical whinings that characterize other branches of magick.

What is unique about Enochian Magick is the absence of such infantile nonsense. Calls are addressed in the language of the beings involved. There is a simple hierarchy that needs to be recognized. The rest is between you and the Angels.

To make matters even simpler he provides us with five flawlessly constructed "Temple Openings" which are inserted prior to the First, Third, Fourth, Fifth and Sixth Keys. By performing the "Temple Openings" prior to reciting the Calls you will find almost half your work done. If you are unclear as to the appropriate signs, pentagrams or hexagrams used in the Temple Openings refer to the Appendices.

The simple procedure outlined below will take you anywhere you wish to go with the system. Of course you are free to expand and innovate upon the system as much as you feel necessary. (I would not, however, advise that you *omit* any of the following steps.)

PRELIMINARY CONSIDERATIONS
TEMPLE ARRANGEMENTS

These can be as simple or as elaborate as you wish. A clean, uncluttered room with an altar or table in the center is perfectly adequate. You may wish to place your Elemental Tablets on the walls of the four quarters (*Air* in the East, *Fire* in the South, *Water* in the West, and *Earth* in the North) or you may wish to arrange them upon the altar. It is not essential to have any Tablets in the Temple at all.

DIRECTIONS OF THE WORKING

When invoking, that is when you wish to bring the Spirit to you, face the *micro*-cosmic-elemental direction dictated by the four winds: operations of *Air* in the East, *Fire* in the South, *Water* in the West, and *Earth* in the North.

When you wish to visit the Spirit in its own world you face the *macro*-cosmic-elemental direction dictated by the Zodiac: operations of *Fire* in the East (Aries), *Earth* in the South (Capricorn), *Air* in the West (Libra), and *Water* in the North (Cancer).

For workings of the Thirty Æthyrs it does not matter which direction you are facing.

DETERMINE THE HIERARCHY
OF THE SPIRIT IN QUESTION

Remember the Temple Openings contain the invocations of the Three Holy Names of God and the Great Elemental King. *It is necessary for you to repeat these names in subsequent invocations.*

STEP ONE
PERFORM THE LESSER
BANISHING RITUAL OF THE PENTAGRAM

This is found in Appendix II. Any magical operation, no matter how simple, should be preceded by a Lesser Banishing Ritual of the Pentagram.

STEP TWO
OPEN THE TEMPLE AND RECITE
THE APPROPRIATE CALL

Note: Remember, all Temple Openings are found in the text of *Chanokh* just prior to the appropriate Call.

EXAMPLE ONE

To invoke **EHNB** from the Tablet of Union:

1. Open the Temple with the Opening of the Portal of the Vault of the Adepts.
2. Recite The First Key and The Second Key.
3. Recite Enochian Conjuration *(see below)* inserting the Angel Name, **EHNB**.

EXAMPLE TWO

To invoke **EXARP** from the Tablet of Union:

1. (Repeat 1 and 2 above.) Open the Temple with The Opening of the Temple in the Grade of $2° = 9°$.
2. Recite The Third Key.
3. Recite Enochian Conjuration *(see below)* inserting the Angel Name, **EXARP**.

EXAMPLE THREE

To invoke the Kerubic Angel **TAAD** from the Air Subangle of the Water Tablet:

1. Open the Temple with The Opening of the Temple in the Grade of 3° = 8°.
2. Recite The Fourth Key (to open the Water Tablet).
3. Recite The Tenth Key (to open the Subangle of Air).
4. Recite Enochian Conjuration (see below) inserting the Angel Name, **TAAD,** the names of the six Seniors of the Water Tablet: **SAIINOV, SOAIZNT, LAOAZRP, LIGDISA, SLGAIOL, LSRAHPM** and the Divine Names of the Calvary Cross, **OLGOTO** and **AALCO**.

EXAMPLE FOUR

To invoke the Lesser Angel **ACCA** from the Fire Subangle of the Air Tablet:

1. Open the Temple with The Opening of the Temple in the Grade of 2° = 9°.
2. Recite The Third Key (to open the Air Tablet).
3. Recite The Ninth Key (to open the Subangle of Fire).
4. Recite Enochian Conjuration (see below) inserting the Angel Name, **ACCA,** the names of the six Seniors of the Air Tablet: **AAOXAIF, AVTOTAR, HTMORDA, HIPOTGA, AHAOZPI, HABIORO** and the Divine Names of the Calvary Cross, **AOURRZ** and **ALOAI** and Kerubic Ruler **XGZD**.

ENOCHIAN CONJURATION

The conjuration that follows was extracted from Crowley's Enochian translation of the First Conjuration of the Goetia. Simply insert the name of the Spirit you wish to work with, and *any* and *all* the names of its hierarchial superiors.

IN ENOCHIAN

Ol vinu od zodakame, Ilasa, Gahe
(Insert Angel Name)
od elanusahe vaoresagi Iaida,
gohusa pujo ilasa, darebesa!
Do-o-i-ape____od____od____od____od____
(use as many names as necessary)
Ol vinu-ta od zodameta,
Ilasa, Gahe (Insert Angel Name)

IN ENGLISH

I invoke and move thee, O thou, Spirit ____
and being exalted above ye in the power of the
Most High, I say unto thee, obey!
In the name of ____and____and____and____and____
I do invoke and by invoking conjure thee,
O thou, Spirit ____.

Now set to work skrying. Keep paper and pencil handy. Some prefer to have a tape recorder running. It is important to maintain some level of objective consciousness. If you fall asleep you are likely to forget your vision and may run into unpleasant complications.

If you run into any "spiritual" characters that make you feel uncomfortable, test them first with the Holy Names from the Tablet you are working with or (in the case of the Thrity Æthyrs), the names of the Governors. If you are still having difficulties, draw the appropriate Banishing Pentagram (see Appendix II for Banishing Pentagrams) and withdraw from the vision.

Do not tire yourself. When you feel fatigued, find an opportunity to withdraw from the vision and Banish.

STEP THREE
CLOSE THE TEMPLE WITH THE
BANISHING RITUAL OF THE PENTAGRAM

I have found the Enochian system to be the safest, cleanest and most logical system of practical magick one can perform. But it is an art and, as such, requires not only study and practice, but also inspiration and the love-hate relationship all artists have with their craft. It is my hope that our book has given you something to study, practice and inspire you.

Chapter Five

Liber LXXXIV vel Chanokh*

A BRIEF ABSTRACT OF THE SYMBOLIC
REPRESENTATION OF THE UNIVERSE DERIVED BY
DOCTOR JOHN DEE THROUGH THE SKRYING OF
SIR EDWARD KELLY

PART I

The Skryer obtained from certain Angels a series of seven talismans. These, grouped about the Holy Twelvefold Table, similarly obtained, were part of the furniture of the Holy Table, as shewn in Plate I. Other appurtenances of this table will be described hereafter.

II

Other Pantacles were obtained in a similar manner. Here (Plate II) is the principal one, which, carved in wax, was placed upon the top of the table. On four others stood the feet of the table.

Note first the Holy Sevenfold Table containing seven Names of God which not even the Angels are able to pronounce.

SAAI $\frac{21}{8}$ EME
BTZKASE[30]
HEIDENE
DEIMOL[30]**A**
I[26]**MEGCBE**
ILAOI $\frac{21}{8}$ VN
IHRLAAL $\frac{21}{8}$

These names are seen written without the heptagram within the heptagon.

---

* Liber LXXXIV vel Chanokh was first published in *The Equinox* Vol. I, Nos. VII and VIII (1912).

By reading these obliquely are obtained names of Angels called—
(1) Filiæ Bonitatis or Filiolæ Lucis.
E, Me, Ese, Iana, Akele, Azdobn, Stimcul
(2) Filii Lucis.
I, Ih, Ilr, Dmal, Heeoa, Beigia, Stimcul
[These are given attributions to the Metals of the Planets in this order: Sol, Luna, Venus, Jupiter, Mars, Mercury, Saturn.]
(3) Filiæ Filiorum Lucis.
S, Ab, Ath, Ized, Ekiei, Madimi, Esemeli
(4) Filii Filiorum Lucis.
L (EL), Aw, Ave, Liba, Iocle, Hagone(l) Ilemese
See all these names in the heptagram of the great seal.

So also there are Seven Great Angels formed thus: take the corner letter S, then the diagonal next to it AB, then the next diagonal ATH, the fourth diagonal, where is I with $^{21}/_8$ (which indicates EL), and we have the name—
SABATHIEL
Continuing the process, we get: **ZEDEKIEL, MADIMIEL, SEMELIEL, NOGAHEL, CORABIEL, LEVANAEL.**

These names will be found in the Pentagram and about it.

These angels are the angels of the Seven Circles of Heaven.

These are but a few of the mysteries of this great seal **SIGILLVM DEI ÆMETH.**

III

The Shew-stone, a crystal which Dee alleged to have been brought to him by angels, was then placed upon this table, and the principal result of the ceremonial skrying of Sir Edward Kelly is the obtaining of the following diagrams, Plate III-VIII.

He symbolized the Fourth-Dimensional Universe in two dimensions as a square surrounded by 30 concentric circles (the 30 Æthyrs or Aires) whose radii increase in a geometrical proportion.

The sides of the square are the four great Watch-Towers (Plates IV-VII) which are attributed to the elements. There is also a "black cross" (or "central tablet" according to the arrangement shewn—compare the black cross bordering the tablets in Plate III with Plate VIII).

Plate III gives the general view.

[The reversed letters which form the word PARAOAN are written in Enochian for convenience, as our A and O are not distinguisable reverse from forward.]

Plate IV gives the complete attribution of the Tablet of Air.

The 6th file is called Linea Patris.

The 7th file is called Linea Filii.

The 7th line is called Linea Spiritus Sancti.

The great cross divides the Tablet into four lesser (sub-elemental) Tablets, the left-hand top corner being Air of Air, the right-hand top corner Water of Air, the left-hand bottom corner Earth of Air, the remaining corner Fire of Air.

Each of these lesser Tablets contain a Calvary Cross of ten squares, which governs it.

Plates V, VI, and VII are similar for the other elements.

This is the way in which the names are drawn from the great Tablets. [Examples taken from Water Tablet.]

1. Linea Spiritus Sancti gives the Three Holy Names of God of 3, 4 and 5 letters respectively:

MPH ARSL GAIOL

2. A whorl around the centre of the Tablet gives the name of the Great Elemental King, **RAAGIOSL** [similarly for Air **BATAIVAH**, for Earth **ICZHHCAL**, for Fire **EDLPRNAA**].

3. The 3 lines of the central cross of Father, Son, and Holy Ghost give the names of 6 seniors. [Thus the 4 tablets hold 24 "elders," as stated in the Apocalypse.] They are drawn of seven letters, each from the centre to the sides of the tablet.

Linea Patris, **SAIINOV** and **SOAIZNT**

Linea Filii, **LAOAZRP** and **LIGDISA**

Linea S.S., **SLGAIOL** and **LSRAHPM**

These three sets of names rule the whole tablet, and must be invoked before specializing in the lesser angles of the sub-elements.

4. The Calvary Crosses.

The name upon the cross read vertically is the name which calls forth the powers of the lesser angle.

NELAPR (water of water)
OLGOTA (air of water)
MALADI (earth of water)
IAAASD (fire of water)

The name read horizontally on the cross is that which compels the evoked force to obedience.

OMEBB (water of water)
AALCO (air of water)
OCAAD (earth of water)
ATAPA (fire of water)

5. Above the bar of the Calvary Cross remain in each case four squares. These are alloted to the Kerubim, who must next be invoked. They are:

TDIM
DIMT
IMTD
MTDI

being metatheses of these four letters. The initial determines the file governed; *e.g.*, **TDIM** governs the file which reads **T(o)ILVR**. These angels are most mighty and benevolent. They are ruled by names of God formed by prefixing the appropriate letter from the "black cross" to their own names.

6. Beneath the bar of the Calvary Cross remain 16 squares not yet accounted for. Here, beneath the presidency of the Kerubim, rule four mighty and benevolent angels—

INGM
LAOC
VSSN
RVOI

7. Triliteral names of demons or elementals are to be formed from these 16 squares, uniting the two letters on either side of the upright of the cross with a letter chosen from the Central Tablet or black cross in accordance with rules which will be given in their due place. Thus: **GM, IN, OC, LA** et cetera, form bases for these triliteral names.

The following rules explain how the sides of the pyramids of which the squares are formed are attributed to the Sephiroth, Planets, Elements, and Zodiacal signs.

1. Great Central Cross. This has 36 squares, for the decanates of the Zodiac.

On the left side of the Pyramid, Linea Partis has the Cardinal signs, the sign of the Element itself at the top, in the order of Tetragrammaton (Fire, Water, Air, Earth) going upwards.

Linea Filii has the Common signs in the same order.

Linea S.S. has the Kerubic signs, that of the element on the left, in the same order, right to left.

But the order of the decans in each sign is reverse, and thus the planets which fill the right-hand side of the Pyramids go in the first two cases downwards, and in the third from left to right.

The upper sides of the Pyramids are all attributed to the Element of Spirit, the lower sides to the Element of the Tablet.

Each square is also referred to the small card of the Tarot which corresponds to the Decan (see 777).

2. Calvary Crosses.

Each has 10 squares.

The upper sides of the Pyramids are uniformly given to Spirit, the lower sides to the Sephiroth, in the order shewn. The left-hand sides are attributed to the Element of the Tablet, the right-hand sides to the sub-element of the lesser angle.

3. Kerubic Squares.

The upper sides pertain to the Element of the Tablet, the lower sides to the sub-element. Right and left-hand sides in this case correspond, according to a somewhat complex rule which it is necessary to give here. The attributions to the Court Cards of the Tarot naturally follow.

4. Lesser Squares.

The upper side of each Pyramid is governed by the Kerub standing on the pile above it. The lower side is governed by the Kerub also, but in order descending as they are from right to left above. [See angle of Air of Water; the Kerubs go Earth, Fire, Water, Air (from the square marked D, the fifth from the left in the top rank of the Tablet), and downward the lower sides of the squares mared O, D. *E, Z (*this should probably read* O, D, X, Z. *Ed.*) go Earth, Fire, Water, Air.]

The left-hand side refers to the Element of the Tablet, the right-hand side to the sub-element of the lesser angle.

5. The Black Cross of Central Tablet.
The upper and lower sides are equally attributed to Spirit.
The left-hand sides to the element of the file, in this order form left to right: Spirit, Air, Water, Earth, Fire.
The right-hand sides to the element of the rank in this order: Air, Water, Earth, Fire.

IV

Follows Plate IX, the Alphabet in which all this is written. It is the Alphabet of the Angelic Language. The invocations which we possess in that tongue follow in their due place.

[It is also called Enochian, as these angels claimed to be those which conversed with the "patriarch Enoch" of Jewish fable.]

V

The Thirty Æthyrs or Aires and their divisions and angels are as follows [We omit for the present consideration of the parts of the earth to which they are stated to correspond, and the question of the attributions to the cardinal points and the Tribes of Israel. These are duly tabulated in Dee's *Liber Scientiæ, Auxilii, et Victoriæ Terrestris*]:

Name of Aire	Names of Governor	Numbers of Servitors	In All
1. LIL.	OCCODON	7209	
	PASCOMB	2360	
	VALGARS	5362	14,931
2. ARN.	DOAGNIS	3636	
	PACASNA	2362	
	DIALIVA	8962	15,960
3. ZOM.	SAMAPHA	4400	
	VIROOLI	3660	
	ANDISPI	9236	17,296
4. PAZ.	THOTANF	2360	
	AXZIARG	3000	
	POTHNIR	6300	11,660
5. LIT.	LAZDIXI	8630	
	NOCAMAL	2306	
	TIARPAX	5802	16,736

Name of Aire	Names of Governor	Numbers of Servitors	In All
6. MAZ.	SAXTOMP	3620	
	VAVAAMP	9200	
	ZIRZIRD	7220	20,040
7. DEO.	OBMACAS	6363	
	GENADOL	7706	
	ASPIAON	6320	20,389
8. ZID.	ZAMFRES	4362	
	TODNAON	7236	
	PRISTAC	2302	13,900
9. ZIP.	ODDIORG	9996	
	CRALPIR	3620	
	DOANZIN	4230	17,846
10. ZAX.	LEXARPH	8880	
	COMANAN	1230	
	TABITOM	1617	11,727

[Note that these 3 names come from the black cross, with the addition of an L. This L is one of the 8 reversed letters in the four watchtowers, the other seven forming the word **PARAOAN**, *q.v. infra.*]

11. ICH.	MOLPAND	3472	
	VANARDA	7236	
	PONODOL	5234	15,942
12. LOE.	TAPAMAL	2658	
	GEDOONS	7772	
	AMBRIAL	3391	13,821
13. ZIM.	GECAOND	8111	
	LAPARIN	3360	
	DOCEPAX	4213	15,684
14. VTA.	TEDOOND	2673	
	VIVIPOS	9236	
	OOANAMB	8230	20,139

Name of Aire	Names of Governor	Numbers of Servitors	In All
15. OXO.	TAHANDO	1367	
	NOCIABI	1367	
	TASTOXO	1886	4,620
16. LEA.	COCARPT	9920	
	LANACON	9230	
	SOCHIAL	9240	28,390
17. TAN.	SIGMORF	7623	
	AYDROPT	7132	
	TOCARZI	2634	17,389
18. ZEN.	NABAOMI	2346	
	ZAFASAI	7689	
	YALPAMB	9276	19,311
19. POP.	TORZOXI	6236	
	ABAIOND	6732	
	OMAGRAP	2388	15,356
20. KHR.	ZILDRON	3626	
	PARZIBA	7629	
	TOTOCAN	3634	14,889
21. ASP.	CHIRSPA	5536	
	TOANTOM	5635	
	VIXPALG	5658	16,929
22. LIN.	OZIDAIA	2232	
	PARAOAN	2326	
	CALZIRG	2367	6,925
23. TOR.	RONOAMB	7320	
	ONIZIMP	7262	
	ZAXANIN	7333	21,915
24. NIA.	ORCAMIR	8200	
	CHIALPS	8360	
	SOAGEEL	8236	24,796

Name of Aire	Names of Governor	Numbers of Servitors	In All
25. VTI.	MIRZIND	5632	
	OBUAORS	6333	
	RANGLAM	6236	18,201
26. DES.	POPHAND	9232	
	NIGRANA	3620	
	BAZCHIM	5637	18,489
27. ZAA.	SAZIAMI	7220	
	MATHVLA	7560	
	ORPAMB	7263	22,043
28. BAG.	LABNIXP	2360	
	FOCISNI	7236	
	OXLOPAR	8200	18,066
29. RII.	VASTRIM	9632	
	ODRAXTI	4236	
	GOMZIAM	7635	21,503
30. TEX.	TAONGLA	4632	
	GEMNIMB	9636	
	ADVORPT	7632	
	DOZINAL	5632	27,532

Plate X. shows us the names of these governors in the four Watch-Towers. Compare with Plate III.

Note that the sigil of each Governor is unique; the four sigils at the corners of Plate X without the great square are those of the four great Elemental Kings:

Air **TAHAOELOJ**
Water **THAHEBYOBEEATAN**
Earth **THAHAAOTAHE**
Fire **OHOOOHAATAN**

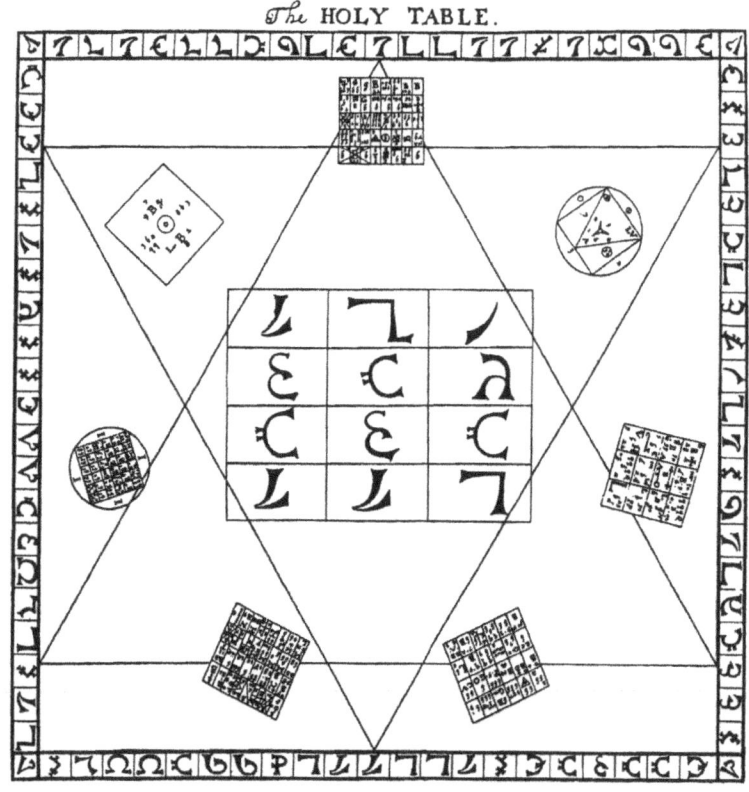

PLATE I.

SIGILLVM DEI ÆMETH.

PLATE II.

THE FOUR GREAT WATCH-TOWERS AND
THE BLACK CROSS WITHIN GENERAL VIEW.

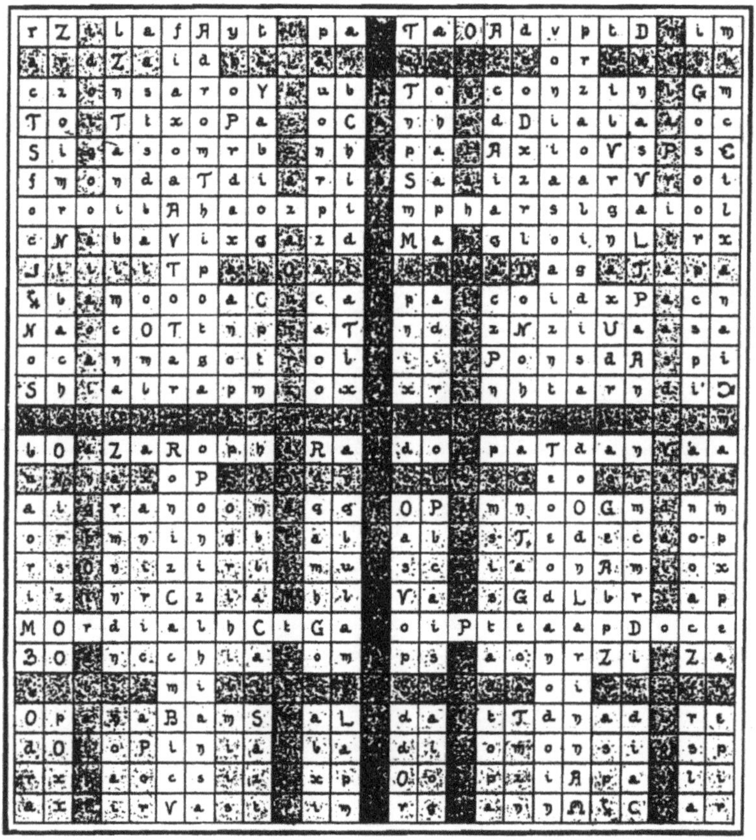

PLATE III.

THE GREAT WATCH-TOWER OF THE EAST, ATTRIBUTED TO AIR.

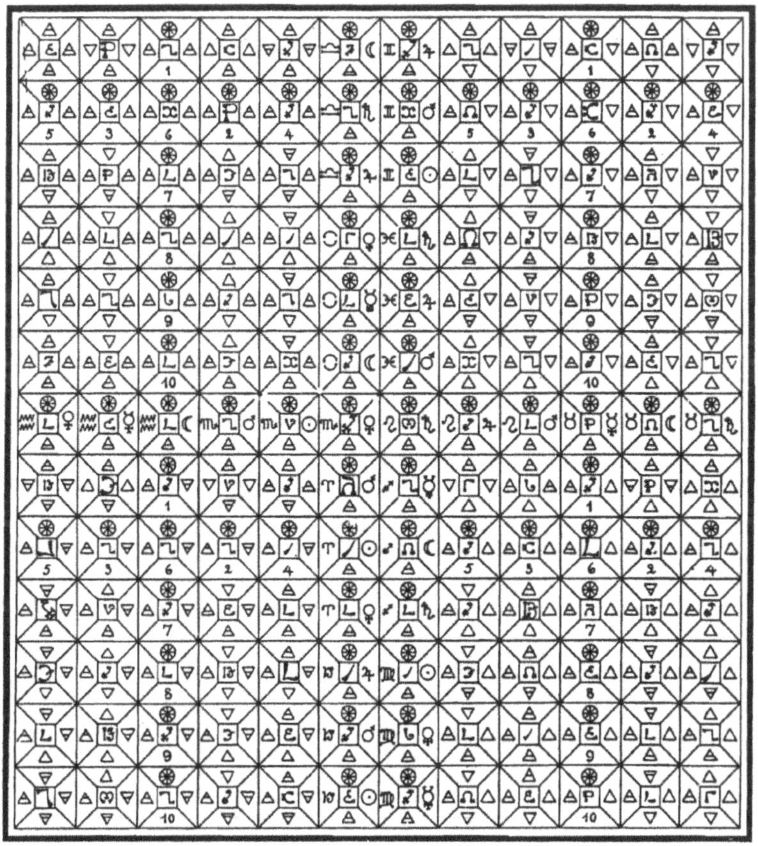

PLATE IV.

THE GREAT WATCH-TOWER OF THE WEST, ATTRIBUTED TO WATER.

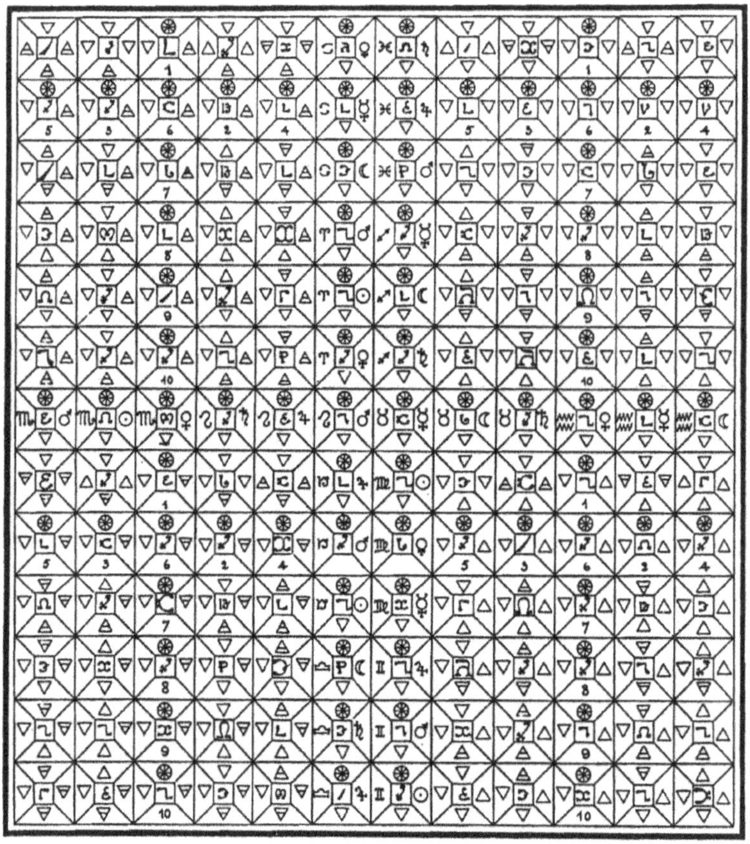

PLATE V.

THE GREAT WATCH-TOWER OF THE NORTH, ATTRIBUTED TO EARTH.

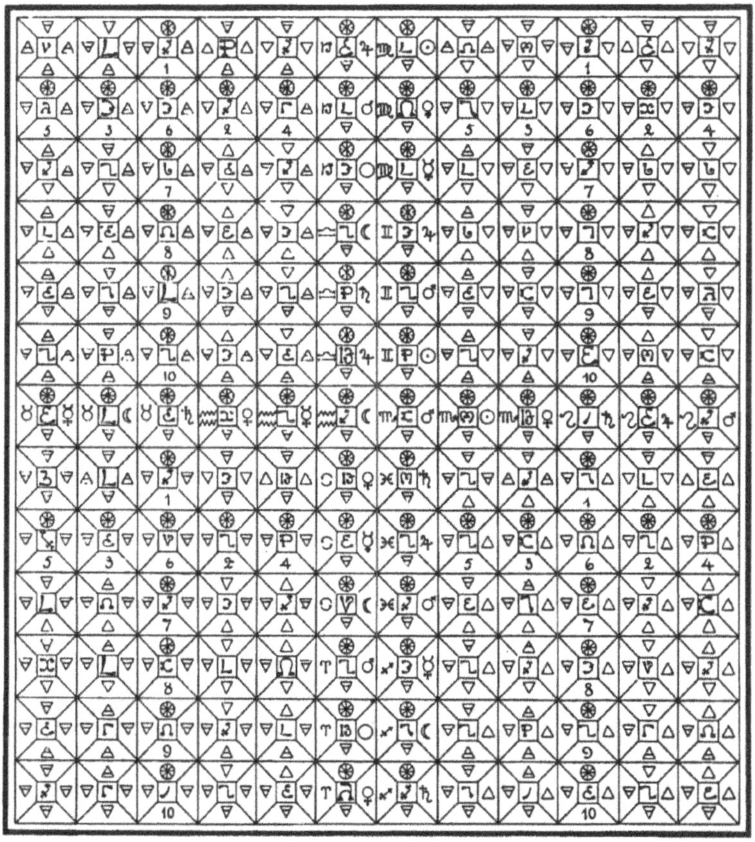

PLATE VI.

THE GREAT WATCH-TOWER OF THE SOUTH, ATTRIBUTED TO FIRE.

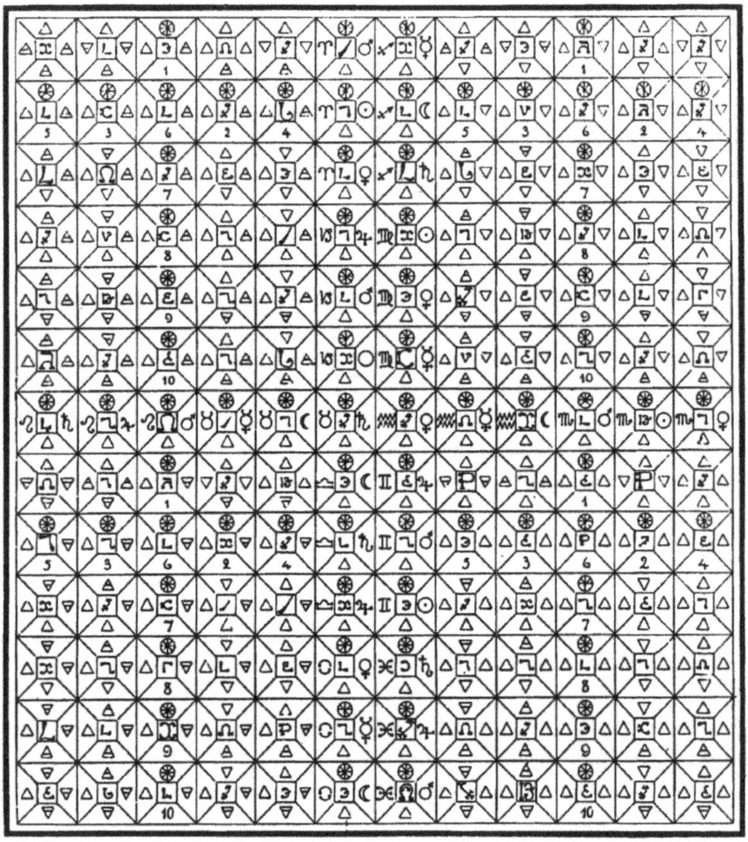

PLATE VII.

THE BLACK CROSS, OR TABLE OF UNION, ATTRIBUTED TO SPIRIT.

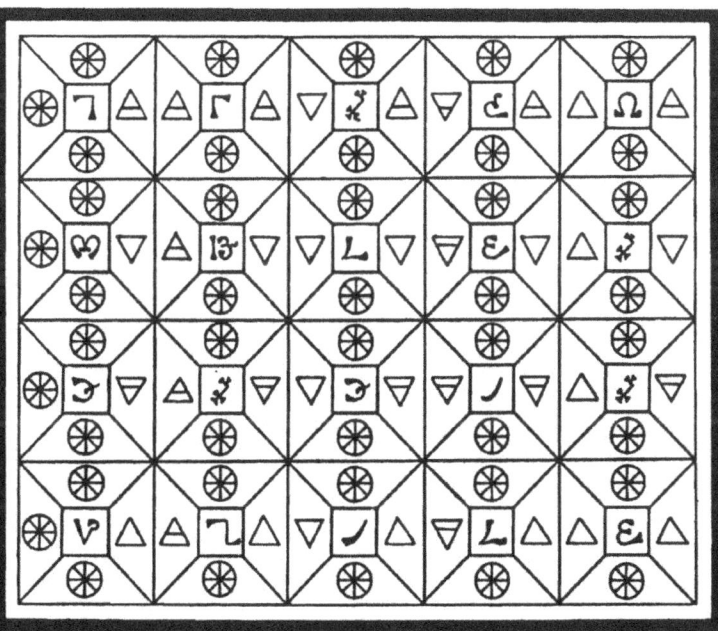

PLATE VIII.

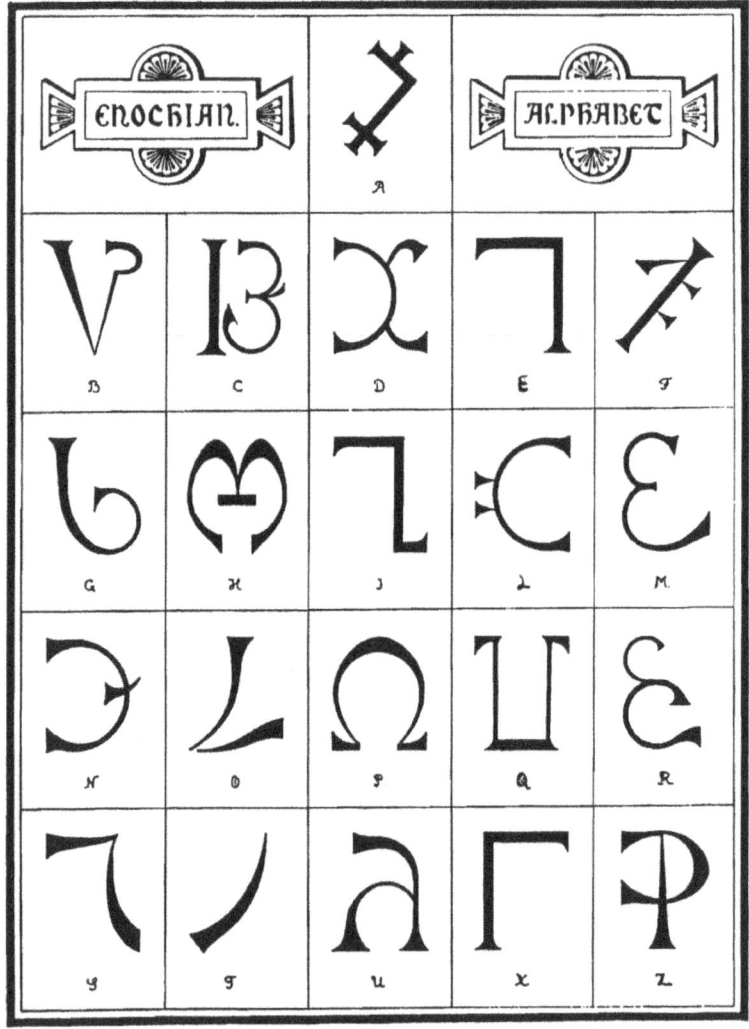

PLATE IX.

PLATE X.

PART II

THE FORTY-EIGHT CALLS OR KEYS

These are Most Solemn Invocations. Use these only after other invocations. Key tablet hath 6 calls, 1 above other 5.

1: Governs generally as a whole the Tablet of Union. Use it *first* in all invocations of Angels of that tablet, but not at all with other 4 tablets.

2: Used as an invocation of Angels e h n b representing governance of Spirit in the Tablet of Union: also precedes, *in the second place*, all invocations of Key tablet Angels. Not used in invocations of 4 other tablets.

3, 4, 5, 6: Used in invocations of Angels of Tablet of Union, *also* of angels of 4 terrestrial tablets, thus —

3: Used to invoke Angels of the letters of the line e x a r p.

For those of Tablet ORO as a whole and for the lesser angle of this tablet, which is that of the element itself, viz. i d o i go. So for others —

The remaining 12 Keys refer to the remaining lesser angles of the tablets, the order of the elements being Air, Water, Earth, Fire.

Pronounce Elemental language (also called Angelic or Enochian) by inserting the next following Hebrew vowel between consonants, *e.g.* e after b (bEth), i after g (gImel), a after d, etc.

THE OPENING OF THE PORTAL OF THE VAULT OF THE ADEPTS

PAROKETH, the Veil of the Sanctuary.
The Sign of Rending of the Veil.
The Sign of the Closing of the Veil.
[Give these.]
Making the Invoking Pentagrams of Spirit.
In the number 21, in the grand word AHIH;
In the Name YHShVH, in the Pass Word I.N.R.I.,

O Spirits of the Tablet of Spirit,
Ye, ye, I invoke!
The sign of Osiris slain!
The sign of the mourning of Isis!
The sign of Apophis and Typhon!
The sign of Osiris Risen!
L.V.X., Lux. The Light of the Cross.
[Give these.]

In the name of IHVH ALVH VDOTh, I declare that the
Spirits of Spirit have been duly invoked.
The Knock 1—4444.

THE FIRST KEY[1]

OL sonuf vaoresaji, gohu IAD Balata, elanusaha caelazod: sobrazod-ol Roray i ta nazodapesed, Giraa ta maelpereji, das hoel-qo qaa notahoa zodimezod, od comemahe ta nobeloha zodien; soba tahil ginonupe pereje aladi, das vaurebes obolehe giresam. Casarem ohorela caba Pire: das zodonurenusagi cab: erem Iadanahe. Pilahe farezodem zodenurezoda adana gono Iadapiel das home-tohe: soba ipame lu ipamis: das sobolo vepe zodomeda poamal, od bogira aai ta piape Piamoel od Vaoan[2]! Zodacare, eca, od zodameranu! odo cicale Qaa; zodoreje, lape zodiredo, Noco Mada, Hoathahe I A I D A!
86 words in this Enochian Call.
[Invokes the whole Tablet of Spirit.]

THE FIRST KEY

I REIGN over ye, saith the God of Justice, in power exalted above the Firmament of Wrath, in whose hands the Sun is as a sword, and the Moon as a through thrusting Fire: who measureth your Garments in the midst of my Vestures, and trussed you together as the palms of my hands. Whose seats I garnished

---
[1] Collation of the various MSS. of these calls has not done away with Various Readings; and there is not enough of the language extant to enable a settlement on general principles.—Ed.
[2] Read here Vooan in invocations of Fallen Spirits.

with the Fire of Gathering, and beautified your garments with admiration. To whom I made a law to govern the Holy Ones, and delivered ye a Rod, with the Ark of Knowledge. Moreover you lifted up your voices and sware obedience and faith to Him that liveth and triumpheth: whose beginning is not, nor end cannot be: which shineth as a flame in the midst of your palaces, and reigneth amongst you as the balance of righteousness and truth!
Move therefore, and shew yourselves! Open the mysteries of your creation! Be friendly unto me, for I am the Servant of the same your God: the true worshipper of the Highest!
(169 words in the English Call.)

THE SECOND KEY

ADAGITA vau-pa-ahe zodonugonu fa-a-ipe salada! Vi-i-vau el! Sobame ial-pereji i-zoda-zodazod pi-adapehe casarema aberameji ta ta-labo paracaleda qo-ta lores-el-qo turebesa ooge balatohe! Giui cahisa lusada oreri od micalapape cahisa bia ozodonugonu! lape noanu tarofe coresa tage o-quo maninu IA-I-DON. Torezodu! gohe-el, zodacare ece ca-no-quoda! zodameranu micalazodo od ozadazodame vaurelar; lape zodir IOIAD!

THE SECOND KEY

CAN the Wings of the Wind understand your voices of Wonder? O you! the second of the First! whom the burning flames have framed in the depth of my Jaws! Whom I have prepared as cups for a wedding, or as the flowers in their beauty for the chamber of Righteousness! Stronger are your feet than the barren stone: and mightier are your voices than the manifold winds! For you are become a building such as is not, save the Mind of the All-Powerful.
Arise, saith the First: Move therefore unto his servants! Shew yourselves in power, and make me a strong Seer-of-things: for I am of Him that liveth for ever!
[Invokes: The File of Spirit in the Tablet of Spirit.
    E — the Root of the Powers of Air.
    H — the Root of the Powers of Water.
    N — the Root of the Powers of Earth.
    B — the Root of the Powers of Fire.
       the Four Aces.]

THE OPENING OF THE TEMPLE IN THE GRADE OF $2° = 9°$.

GIVE the Sign of Shu.

[Knock.] Let us adore the Lord and King of Air! Shaddai El Chai! Almighty and ever-living One, be Thy Name ever magnified in the Life of All. (Sign of Shu.) Amen!

[Make the Invoking Pentagram of Spirit Active in these names: AHIH AGLA EXARP.]

[Make the Invoking Pentagram of Air in these names: IHVH ShDI AL ChI.]

And Elohim said: Let us make Adam in Our own image, after our likeness, and let them have dominion over the fowls of the air.

In the Names of IHVH and of ShDI AL ChI, Spirits of Air, Adore your Creator!

[With air-dagger (or other suitable weapon) make the sign of Aquarius.] In the name of RPAL and in the Sign of the Man, Spirits of Air, adore your Creator!

[Make the Cross.] In the Names and Letters of the Great Eastern Quadrangle, Spirits of Air, Adore your Creator!

[Hold dagger aloft.] In the Three great Secret Names of God, ORO IBAH AOZPI that are borne upon the Banners of the East, Spirits of Air, adore your Creator!

[Again elevate dagger.] In the Name of BATAIVAH, great King of the East, Spirits of Air, adore your Creator!

In the Name of Shaddai AL Chai, I declare that the Spirits of Air have been duly invoked.

The Knock 333—333—333.

THE THIRD KEY

MICAMA! goho Pe-IAD! zodir com-selahe azodien biabe oslon-dohe. Norezoda cahisa otahila Gigipahe; vaunud-el-cahisa tapu-ime qo-mos-pelehe telocahe; qui-i-inu toltoregi cahisa i cahisaji em ozodien; dasata beregida od torezodul! Ili e-Ol balazodareji, od aala tahilanu-os netaabe: daluga vaomesareji elonusa cape-miali vaoresa *cala* homila; cocasabe fafenu izodizodope, od miinoagi de ginetaabe: vaunu na-na-e-el: panupire malapireji caosaji. Pilada noanu vaunalahe balata od-vaoan. Do-o-i-ape mada: goholore, gohus, amiranu! Micama! Yehusozod ca-ca-com, od do-o-a-inu noari micaolazoda a-ai-om. Casaremji gohia: Zodacare! Vaunigilaji! od im-ua-mar pugo pelapeli Ananael Qo-a-an.

(Eighty words in the Enochian Call.)

THE THIRD KEY

BEHOLD! saith your God! I am a circle on whose hands stand Twelve Kingdoms. Six are the seats of living breath: the rest are as sharp Sickles, or the Horns of Death. Wherein the creatures of Earth are and are not, except (in) mine own hands; which sleep and shall rise!

In the First I made ye stewards, and placed ye in twelve seats of government: giving unto every one of you power successively over the 456 true ages of time: to the intent that from the highest vessels and the corners of your governments you might work my Power, pouring down the fires of life and increase continually on the earth. Thus you are become the skirts of Justice and Truth.

In the name of the same your God, lift up, I say, yourselves!

Behold! His mercies flourish, and (His) Name is become mighty among us. In whom we say: Move! Descend! and apply yourselves unto us as unto the partakers of His Secret Wisdom in your Creation.

(167 words in this English Call.)

> [Invokes: EXARP, the whole tablet of Air.
> The angle of Air of Air.
> The Prince of the Chariot of the Winds.]

THE OPENING OF THE TEMPLE IN THE GRADE OF $3° = 8°$.

GIVE the Sign of Auramoth.

[Knock.] Let us adore the Lord and King of Water! Elohim Tzabaoth! Elohim of Hosts!

Glory be to the Ruach Elohim which moved upon the Face of the Waters of Creation!

AMEN!

[Make the Invoking Pentagram of Spirit Passive and pronounce these names: AHIH AGLA HCOMA.]

[Make the Invoking Pentagram of Water and pronounce: AL ALHIM TzBAVTh.]

And Elohim said: Let us make Adam in Our image; and let

them have dominion over the Fish of the Sea! In the Name of AL, Strong and Powerful, and in the Name of ALHIM TzBAVTh, Spirits of Water, adore your Creator!

[Make Sigil of Eagle with cup.] In the name of GBRIAL and in the sign of the Eagle, Spirits of Water, adore your Creator!

[Make cross with cup.] In all the Names and Letters of the Great Quadrangle of the West, Spirits of Water, adore your Creator!

[Elevate cup.] In the three great Secret Names of God MPH ARSL GAIOL that are borne upon the Banners of the West, Spirits of Water, adore your Creator!

[Elevate cup.] In the Name RAAGIOSEL, great King of the West, Spirits of Water, adore your Creator!

In the name of Elohim Tzabaoth, I declare that the Spirits of Water have been duly invoked.

The Knock. 1—333—1—333.

THE FOURTH KEY

OTAHIL elasadi babaje, od dorepaha gohol: gi-cahisaje auauago coremepe *peda*, dasonuf vi-vau-di-vau? Casaremi oeli *meapeme* sobame agi coremepo carep-el: casaremeji caro-o-dazodi cahisa od vaugeji; dasata ca-pi-mali cahisa ca-pi-ma-on: od elonusahinu cahisa ta el-o *calaa*. Torezodu nor-quasahi od fe-caosaga: Bagile zodir e-na-IAD: das iod apila! Do-o-a-ipe quo-A-AL, zodacare! Zodameranu obelisonugi resat-el aaf nor-mo-lapi!

THE FOURTH KEY

I HAVE set my feet in the South, and have looked about me, saying: are not the thunders of increase numbered 33, which reign in the second Angle?

Under whom I have placed 9639: whom none hath yet numbered, but One; in whom the Second Beginnings of Things are and wax strong, which also successively are the Numbers of Time: and their powers are as the first 456.

Arise! you sons of Pleasure! and visit the earth: for I am the Lord your God; which is and liveth (for ever)! In the name of the Creator, move! and shew yourselves as pleasant deliverers, that you may praise him among the sons of men!

[Invokes: HCOMA, the whole tablet of Water.
The Angle of Water of Water.
The Queen of the Thrones of Water.]

THE OPENING OF THE TEMPLE IN THE GRADE OF 1° = 10°.

GIVE the Sign of the God SET fighting.

Purify with Fire and Water, and announce "The Temple is cleansed."

[Knock.] Let us adore the Lord and King of Earth!

Adonai ha Aretz, Adonai Melekh, unto Thee be the Kingdom, the Sceptre, and the Splendour: Mulkuth, Geburah, Gedulah, The Rose of Sharon and the Lily of the Valley, Amen!

[Sprinkle Salt before Earth Tablet.] Let the Earth adore Adonai!

[Make the Invoking Hexagram of Saturn.]

[Make the Invoking Pentagram of Spirit Passive, and pronounce these Names: AHIH AGLA NANTA.]

[Make the Invoking Pentagram of Earth, and pronounce this Name: ADNI MLK.]

And Elohim said: Let us make Man in Our own image; and let them have dominion over the Fish of the Sea and over the Fowl of the Air: and over every creeping thing that creepeth upon the Earth. And the Elohim created A Th-H-ADAM: in the image of the Elohim created them; male and female created They them. In the Name of ADNI MLK, and of the Bride and Queen of the Kingdom; Spirits of Earth, adore your Creator!

[Make the Sign of Taurus.] In the Name of AVRIAL, great archangel of Earth, Spirits of Earth, adore your Creator!

[Make the Cross.] In the Names and Letters of the Great Northern Quadrangle, Spirits of Earth, adore your Creator!

[Sprinkle water before Earth Tablet.] In the three great secret Names of God, MOR, DIAL, HCTGA, that are borne upon the Banners of the North, Spirits of Earth, adore your Creator!

[Cense the Tablet.] In the Name of IC-ZOD-HEH-CA(L), great King of the North, Spirits of Earth, adore your Creator!

In the Name of Adonai Ha-Aretz, I declare that the Spirits of Earth have been duly invoked.

The Knock. 4444 — 333 — 22 — 1.

THE FIFTH KEY

SAPAHE zodimii du-i-be, od noasa ta qu-a-nis, adarocahe dorepehal caosagi od faonutas peripesol ta-be-liore. Casareme A-me-ipezodi na-zodaretahe *afa*; od dalugare zodizodope zode-lida caosaji tol-toregi; od zod-cahisa esiasacahe El ta-vi-vau; od iao-d tahilada das hubare *pe-o-al*; soba coremefa cahisa ta Ela Vaulasa od Quo-Co-Casabe. Eca niisa od darebesa quo-a-asa; fetahe-arezodi od beliora; ia-ial eda-nasa cicalesa; bagile Ge-iad I-el!

THE FIFTH KEY

THE mighty sounds have entered into the third angle, and are become as olives in the Olive Mount; looking with gladness upon the earth, and dwelling in the brightness of the Heavens as continual Comforters.

Unto whom I fastened 19 Pillars of Gladness, and gave them vessels to water the earth with her creatures; and they are brothers of the First and Second, and the beginning of their own seats, which are garnished with 69,636 ever-burning lamps: whose numbers are the First, the Ends, and the Contents of Time.

Therefore come ye and obey your creation: visit us in peace and comfort: conclude us receivers of your mysteries: for why? Our Lord and Master is the All-One!

[Invokes: NANTA; the whole tablet of Earth.
The angle of Earth of Earth.
The Princess of the Echoing Hills,
the Rose of the Palace of Earth.]

THE OPENING OF THE TEMPLE IN THE GRADE OF $4° = 7°$.

GIVE the Sign of Thoum-aesh-neith.

[Knock.] Let us adore the Lord and King of Fire!

Tetragrammaton Tzabaoth! Blessed be Thou! The Leader of Armies is Thy Name! AMEN!

[Make the Invoking Pentagram of Spirit Active, and pronounce these Names: AHIH AGLA BITOM.]

[Make the Invoking Pentagram of Fire, and pronounce: ALHIM IHVH TzBAVTh.]

[Make the Sign of Leo with censer (or other suitable weapon).] In the Name of Mikal, archangel of Fire, Spirits of Fire, adore your Creator!

[Make the Cross.] In the Names and Letters of the Great Southern Quadrangle, Spirits of Fire, adore your Creator!

[Elevate censer.] In the three Secret names of God, OIP TEAA PDOCE, that are borne upon the banners of the South, Spirits of Fire, adore your Creator!

[Lower and lift censer.] In the Name of EDELPERNA, great King of the South, Spirits of Fire, adore your Creator!

In the Name of IHVH TzBAVTh, I declare that the Spirits of Fire have been duly invoked.

The Knock. 333—1—333.

THE SIXTH KEY

GAHE sa-div cahisa *em*, micalazoda Pil-zodinu, sobam El haraji mir babalonu od obeloce samevelaji, dalagare malapereji ar-caosaji od *acame* canele, sobola zodare fa-beliareda caosaji od cahisa aneta-na miame ta Viv od Da. Daresare Sol-petahe-bienu. Be-ri-ta od zodacame ji-mi-calazodo: sob-ha-atahe tarianu luia-he od ecarinu MADA Qu-a-a-on!

THE SIXTH KEY

THE Spirits of the fourth angle are Nine, Mighty in the Firmament of Waters: whom the First hath planted, a torment to the wicked and a garland to the righteous: giving unto them fiery darts to vanne the Earth, and 7699 continual workmen, whose courses visit with comfort the earth; and are in government and continuance as the Second and the Third—

Therefore hearken unto my voice! I have talked of you, and I move you in power and presence, whose works shall be a song of honour, and the praise of your God in your Creation!

[Invokes BITOM; the whole tablet of Fire.
The Angle of Fire of Fire.
The Lord of the Flame and the Lightning,
The King of the Spirits of Fire.]

THE SEVENTH KEY

RA-ASA isalamanu para-di-zoda oe-cari-mi aao iala-pire-gahe Qui-inu. Enai butamonu od inoasa *ni* pa-ra-diala. Casare-meji ujeare cahirelanu, od zodonace lucifatianu, caresa ta vavale-zodirenu tol-hami. Soba lonudohe od nuame cahisa ta Da o Desa vo-ma-dea od pi-beliare itahila rita od miame ca-ni-quola rita! Zodacare! Zodameranu! Iecarimi Quo-a-dahe od I-mica-ol-zodo-da aaiome. Bajirele papenore idalu-gama elonushi—od umapelifa vau-ge-ji Bijil—IAD!

THE SEVENTH KEY

THE East is a house of Virgins singing praises among the flames of first glory wherein the Lord hath opened his mouth; and they are become 28 living dwellings in whom the strength of man rejoiceth; and they are apparelled with ornaments of brightness, such as work wonders on all creatures. Whose kingdoms and con-tinuance are as the Third and Fourth, strong towers and places of comfort, the Seats of Mercy and Continuance. O ye Servants of Mercy, Move! Appear! Sing praises unto the Creator; and be mighty amongst us. For that to this remembrance is given power, and our strength waxeth strong in our Comforter!
[Invokes The Angle of Water of Air, in the tablet of Air.
The Queen of the Thrones of Air.]

THE EIGHTH KEY

BAZODEMELO i ta pi-ripesonu olanu Na-zodavabebe *ox*. Casaremeji varanu cahisa vaugeji asa berameji balatoha: goho IAD. Soba miame tarianu ta lolacis Abaivoninu od azodiajiere riore. Irejila cahisa da das pa-aox busada Caosago, das chaisa od ipuranu telocahe cacureji o-isalamahe lonucaho od Vovina care-bafe? NIISO! bagile avavago gohon. NIISO! bagile momare si-aionu, od mabezoda IAD oi asa-momare poilape. NIIASA! Zoda-meranu ciaosi caosago od belioresa od coresi ta a beramiji.

THE EIGHTH KEY

THE Midday, the first is as the third Heaven made of 26 Hyacinthine Pillars, in whom the Elders are become strong, which I have prepared for mine own Righteousness, saith the Lord: whose long continuance shall be as bucklers to the Stooping Dragon, and like unto the harvest of a Widow. How many are there which remain in the Glory of the Earth, which are, and shall not see Death until the House fall and the Dragon sink? Come away! for the Thunders (of increase) have spoken. Come away! for the Crowns of the Temple and the Robe of Him that is, was, and shall be, crowned, are divided! Come forth! Appear! to the terror of the Earth, and to our comfort, and to the comfort of such as are prepared.

The Angle of Earth of Air, in the tablet of Air.
The Princess of the Rushing Winds,
The Lotus of the Palace of Air.

THE NINTH KEY

MICAOLI beranusaji perejela napeta ialopore, das barinu efafaje *Pe* vaunupeho olani od obezoda, soba-ca upaahe cahisa tatanu od taranau balie, alare busada so-bolunu od cahisa hoel-qo ca-noquodi *cial*. Vaunesa aladonu mom caosago ta iasa olalore ginai limelala. Amema cahisa sobra madarida zod cahisa! Ooa moanu cahisa avini darilapi caosajinu: od butamoni pareme zodumebi canilu. Dazodisa etahamezoda cahisa dao, od mireka ozodola cahisa pidiai Colalala. Ul ci ninu a sobame ucime. Bajile? IAD BALATOHE cahirelanu pare! NIISO! od upe ofafafe; bajile a-cocasahe icoresaka a uniji beliore.

THE NINTH KEY

A MIGHTY guard of Fire with two-edged swords flaming (which have eight Vials of wrath for two times and a half, whose wings are of wormwood and of the marrow of salt), have set their feet in the West, and are measured with their 9996 ministers. These gather up the moss of the Earth as the rich man doth his Treasure. Cursed are they whose iniquities they are! In their eyes are mill-stones greater than the Earth, and from their mouths run seas of blood. Their heads are covered with diamonds, and upon their heads are marble stones[3] Happy is he on whom they frown not. For

why? The Lord of Righteousness rejoiceth in them! Come away, and not your Vials: for that the time is such as requireth Comfort.
The Angle of Fire of Air, in the tablet of Air.
The Lord of the Winds and Breezes,
The King of the Spirits of Air.

THE TENTH KEY

CORAXO cahisa coremepe, od belanusa Lucala azodiazodore paebe Soba iisononu cahisa uirequo *ope* copehanu od racalire maasi bajile caosagi; das yalaponu dosiji od basajime; od ox ex dazodisa siatarisa od salaberoxa cynuxire faboanu. Vaunala cahisa conusata das *daox* cocasa ol Oanio yore vohima ol jizodyazoda od eoresa cocasaji pelosi molui das pajeipe, laraji same darolanu matorebe cocasaji emena. El pataralaxa yolaci matabe nomiji mononusa olora jinayo anujelareda. Ohyo! ohyo! ohyo! ohyo! ohyo! ohyo! noibe Ohyo! caosagonu! Bajile madarida i zodirope cahiso darisapa! NIISO! caripe ipe nidali!

THE TENTH KEY

THE Thunders of Judgment and Wrath are numbered and are harboured in the North, in the likeness of an Oak whose branches are 22 nests of lamentation and weeping laid up for the earth: which burn night and day, and vomit out the heads of scorpions and live Sulphur mingled with poison. These be the thunders that, 5678 times in the twenty-fourth part of a moment, roar with a hundred mighty earthquakes and a thousand times as many surges, which rest not, neither know any[4] time here. One rock bringeth forth a thousand, even as the heart of man doth his thoughts. Woe! Woe! Woe! Woe! Woe! Woe! Yea Woe be to the Earth, for her iniquity is, was, and shall be great. Come away! but not your mighty sounds!
The Angle of Air of Water, in the tablet of Water.
The Prince of the Chariot of the Waters.

---
[3] v.I. "Upon their hands are marble sleeves."
[4] v.I. "Any echoing time between."

THE ELEVENTH KEY

OXIAYALA holada, od zodirome *O* coraxo das zodiladare raasyo. Od vabezodire cameliaxa od bahala: NIISO! salamanu telocahe! Casaremanu hoel-qo, od ti ta zod cahisa soba coremefa i ga. NIISA! bagile aberameji nonuçape. Zodacare eca od Zodameranu! odo cicale Qaa! Zodoreje, lape zodiredo Noco Mada hoathahe IAIDA!

THE ELEVENTH KEY

THE mighty Seat groaned, and there were five Thunders that flew into the East. And the Eagle spake and cried aloud; Come away from the House of Death! And they gathered themselves together and became (those) of whom it is measured, and it is as They are, whose number is 31. Come away! For I have prepared (a place) for you. Move therefore, and shew yourselves! Unveil the mysteries of your Creation. Be friendly unto me, for I am the servant of the same your God: the true worshipper of the Highest.

The Angle of Earth of Water, in the tablet of Water.

The Princess of the Waters,

the Lotus of the Palace of the Floods.

THE TWELFTH KEY

NONUCI dasonuf Babaje od cahisa *ob* hubaio tibibipe: alalare ataraahe od ef! Darix fafenu *mianu* ar Enayo ovof! Soba dooainu aai i VONUPEHE. Zodacare, gohusa, od Zodameranu. Odo cicale Qaa! Zodoreje, lape zodiredo Noco Mada, hoathahe IAIDA!

THE TWELFTH KEY

O YE that range in the South and are the 28 Lanterns of Sorrow, bind up your girdles and visit us! bring down your train 3663 (servitors), that the Lord may be magnified, whose name amongst ye is Wrath. Move! I say, and shew yourselves! Unveil the mysteries of your Creation. Be friendly unto me, for I am the servant of the same your God, the true worshipper of the Highest.

The Angle of Fire of Water, in the tablet of Water.

The Lord of the Waves and the Waters,

the King of the Hosts of the Sea.

THE THIRTEENTH KEY

NAPEAI Babajehe das berinu *vax* ooaona larinuji vonupehe doalime: conisa olalogi oresaha da cahisa afefa. Micama isaro Mada od Lonu-sahi-toxa, das ivaumeda aai Jirosabe. Zodacare od Zodameranu. Odo cicale Qaa! Zodoreje, lape zodiredo Noco Mada, hoathahe IAIDA.

THE THIRTEENTH KEY

O YE Swords of the South, which have 42 eyes to stir up the wrath of Sin: making men drunken which are empty: Behold the Promise of God, and His Power, which is called amongst ye a bitter sting! Move and Appear! unveil the mysteries of your Creation, for I am the servant of the same your God, the true worshipper of the Highest.

The Angle of Air of Earth, in the tablet of Earth.
The Prince of the Chariot of Earth.

THE FOURTEENTH KEY

NORONI bajihie pasahasa Oiada! das tarinuta mireca *ol* tahila dodasa tolahame caosado *h*omida; das berinu orocahe *quare*: Micama! Bial' Oiad; aisaro toxa das ivame aai Balatima. Zodacare od Zodameranu! Odo cicale Qaa! Zodoreje, lape zodiredo Noco Mada, hoathahe IAIDA.

THE FOURTEENTH KEY

O YE Sons of Fury, the Daughters of the Just One! that sit upon 24 seats, vexing all creatures of the Earth with age, that have 1636 under ye. Behold! The voice of God: the promise of Him who is called amongst ye Fury or Extreme Justice. Move and shew yourselves! Unveil the mysteries of your Creation; be friendly unto me, for I am servant of the same your God: the true worshipper of the Highest!

The Angle of Water of Earth, in the tablet of Earth.
The Queen of the Thrones of Earth.

THE FIFTEENTH KEY

ILASA! tabaanu li-El pereta, casaremanu upaahi cahisa *dareji*; das oado caosaji oresacore: das omaxa monasaçi Baeouibe od emetajisa Iaiadix. Zodacare od Zodameranu! Odo cicale Qaa. Zodoreje, lape zodiredo Noco Mada, hoathahe IAIDA.

THE FIFTEENTH KEY

OH THOU, the Governor of the first Flame, under whose wings are 6739; that weave the Earth with dryness: that knowest the Great Name "Righteousness," and the Seal of Honour. Move and Appear! Unveil the mysteries of your creation; be friendly unto me, for I am the servant of the same your God: the true worshipper of the Highest!

The Angle of Fire of Earth, in the tablet of Earth.
The Lord of the Wide and Fertile Land,
the King of the Spirits of Earth.

THE SIXTEENTH KEY

ILASA viviala pereta! Salamanu balata, das acaro odazodi busada, od belioraxa balita: das inusi caosaji lusadanu *emoda*; das ome od taliobe: darilapa iehe ilasa Mada Zodilodarepe. Zodacare od Zodameranu. Odo cicale Qaa: zodoreje, lape zodiredo Noco Mada, hoathahe IAIDA.

THE SIXTEENTH KEY

O THOU second Flame, the House of Justice, which hast thy beginning in glory and shalt comfort the Just: which walkest upon the Earth with 8763 feet, which understand and separate creatures! Great art thou in the God of Stretch forth and Conquer. Move and appear! Unveil the mysteries of your Creation: be friendly unto me, for I am servant of the same your God, the true worshipper of the Highest.

The Angle of Air of Fire, in the tablet of Fire.
The Prince of the Chariot of Fire.

THE SEVENTEENTH KEY

ILASA dial pereta! soba vaupaahe cahisa nanuba zodixalayo dodasihe od berinuta *faxisa* hubaro tasataxa yolasa: soba Iad *i* Vonupehe o Uonupehe: aladonu dax ila od toatare! Zodacare od Zodameranu! Odo cicale Qaa! Zodoreje, lape zodiredo Noco Mada, hoathahe IAIDA.

THE SEVENTEENTH KEY

O THOU third Flame! whose wings are thorns to stir up vexation, and who hast 7336 living lamps going before Thee: whose God is "Wrath in Anger': Gird up thy loins and hearken! Move and Appear! Unveil the mysteries of your Creation; be friendly unto me, for I am the servant of the same your God, the true worshipper of the Highest.

The Angle of Water of Fire, in the tablet of Fire.
The Queen of the Thrones of Flame.

THE EIGHTEENTH KEY

ILASA micalazoda olapireta ialpereji beliore: das odo Busadire Oiad ouoaresa caosago: casaremeji Laiada *eranu* berinutasa cafafame das ivemeda aqoso adoho Moz, od maof-fasa. Bolape como belioreta pamebeta, Zodacare od Zodameranu! Odo cicale Qaa. Zodoreje, lape zodiredo Noco Mada, hoathahe IAIDA.

THE EIGHTEENTH KEY

O THOU mighty Light and burning Flame of Comfort! that unveilest the Glory of God to the centre of the Earth, in whom the 6332 secrets of Truth have their abiding, that is called in thy kingdom "Joy" and not to be measured. Be thou a window of comfort unto me! Move and Appear! Unveil the mysteries of your Creation; be friendly unto me, for I am the servant of the same your God, the true worshipper of the Highest.

The Angle of Earth of Fire, in the tablet of Fire.
The Princess of the Shining Flame,
the Rose of the Palace of Fire.

MARK WELL!

THESE first 18 calls are in reality 19; that is, 19 in the Celestial Orders; but with us the first table hath no call, and can have no call, seeing that it is of the Godhead. Thus, then, with us hath it the number of 0, though with them that of 1. (Even as the first key of ROTA hath the number 0.)

After this follow the calls or keys of the Thirty Aires or Æthyrs: which are in substance similar, though, in the name of the Æthyrs, diversified.

The titles of the Thirty Æthyrs whose dominion extendeth in ever-widening circles without and beyond the Watch-Towers of the Universe.

(The first is Outermost)

1	LIL	16	LEA
2	ARN	17	TAN
3	ZOM	18	ZEN
4	PAZ	19	POP
5	LIT	20	KHR
6	MAZ	21	ASP
7	DEO	22	LIN
8	ZID	23	TOR
9	ZIP	24	NIA
10	ZAX	25	VTI
11	ICH	26	DES
12	LOE	27	ZAA
13	ZIM	28	BAG
14	UTA	29	RII
15	OXO	30	TEX

THE CALL OR KEY OF THE THIRTY ÆTHYRS

MADARIATZA das perifa LIL[5]cahisa micaolazoda saanire caosago od fifisa balzodizodarasa Iaida. Nonuça gohulime: Micama adoianu MADA faoda beliorebe, soba ooaona cahisa luciftias peripesol, das aberaasasa nonuçafe netaaibe caosaji od tilabe adapehaheta damepelozoda, tooata nonuçafe jimicalazodoma larasada tofejilo marebe yareryo IDOIGO[6] od torezodulape yaodafe gohola, Caosaga, tabaoreda saanire, od caharisateosa yorepoila tiobela busadire, tilable noalanu paida oresaba, od dodaremeni zodayolana. Elazodape tilaba pare meji peripesatza, od ta qurelesata booapisa. Lanibame oucaho sayomepe, od caharisateosa ajitoltorenu, mireca qo tiobela lela. Tonu paomebeda dizodalamo asa pianu, od caharisateosa aji-la-tore-torenu paracahe a sayomepe. Coredazodizoda dodapala od fifalazoda, lasa manada, od faregita bamesa omaoasa. Conisabera od auauotza tonuji oresa; catabela noasami tabejesa leuitahemonuji. Vanucahi omepetilabe oresa! Bagile? Moooable OL coredazodizoda. El capimao itzomatzipe, od caocasabe gosaa. Bajilenu pi tianuta a babalanuda, od faoregita teloca uo uime.

Madariiatza, torezodu!!! Oadariatza orocaha aboaperi! Tabaori periazoda aretabasa! Adarepanu coresata dobitza! Yolacame periazodi arecoazodiore, od quasabe qotinuji! Ripire paaotzata sagacore! Umela od peredazodare cacareji Aoiveae coremepeta! Torezodu! Zodacare od Zodameranu, asapeta sibesi butamona das surezodasa Tia balatanu. Odo cicale Qaa, od Ozodazodama pelapeli IADANAMADA!

THE CALL OR KEY OF THE THIRTY ÆTHYRS

O YE Heavens which dwell in the First Aire, ye are mighty in the parts of the Earth, and execute the Judgment of the Highest! Unto you it is said: Behold the Face of your God, the beginning of Comfort, whose eyes are the brightness of the Heavens,which provided you for the Government of the Earth, and her unspeakable variety, furnishing you with the power of understanding to dispose all things according to the Providence of Him that sitteth on the

---
[5] Or other Aire as may be willed.
[6] This name may be appropriately varied with the Aire.

Holy Throne, and rose up in the Beginning, saying: The Earth, let her be governed by her parts, and let there be Division in her, that the glory of her may be always drunken, and vexed in itself. Her course, let it run with the Heavens; and as an handmaid let her serve them. One season, let it confound another, and let there be no creature upon or within her the same. All her members, let them differ in their qualities, and let there be no one Creature equal with another. The reasonable Creatures of the Earth, and Men, let them vex and weed out one another; and their dwelling-places, let them forget their Names. The work of man and his pomp, let them be defaced. His buildings, let them become Caves for beasts of the Field! Confound her understanding with darkness! For why? it repenteth me that I have made Man. One while let her be known, and another while a stranger: because she is the bed of an Harlot, and the dwelling-place of him that is fallen.

O ye Heavens, arise! The lower heavens beneath you, let them serve you! Govern those that govern! Cast down such as fall. Bring forth with those that increase, and destroy the rotten. No place let it remain in one number. Add and diminish until the stars be numbered. Arise! Move! and appear before the Covenant of His mouth, which He hath sworn unto us in His Justice. Open the Mysteries of your Creation, and make us partakers of THE UNDEFILED KNOWLEDGE.

Finished are the Calls or Keys.

The Three Mighty Names of God Almighty
coming forth from
The Thirty Æthyrs

The First Name—
LAZodaPeLaMeDaZodaZODaZodILaZodUOLaTa ZodaPe-KALaTaNuVaDaZodaBeReTa.
The Second Name—
IROAIAEIIAKOITaXEAEOHeSIOIITEAAIE.
The Third Name—
LaNuNuZodaTaZodODaPeXaHEMAOANuNuPe RePeNu-RAISAGIXa.

Ended are the Forty-eight Calls or Keys.

Chapter Six

Divine Eroticism

Intimate union of the worshipper with the Divine Principal is a central theme of religion. It is quite natural that the images which are evoked by the Devotee in his ardor for the Beloved are identical or similar to those that accompany sexual longings. The traditional cultures of India and the Orient, of Africa, Polynesia, of the natives of North and South America, indeed of almost any culture unpolluted by Judeo-Christian-Islamic thought, have no difficulty whatsoever with this parallel.

With the exception of the *Song of Solomon*, Western religious literature avoids Divine Eroticism like the plague. Even the esoteric disciplines of the West seem uncomfortable with the subject and go to great lengths to veil their terms. The bizarre nomenclature of Alchemy, when studied with half your brain in the bedroom, reveals that perhaps there are several good reasons why the alchemists were called "puffers". But for the most part, we in the West are expected to unite with our Divine Beloved vicariously.

Nuns are the "Brides of Christ", we unite with the Father or Mother only "through the Son." Even the "magic" ceremony needed to consummate these voyeuristic unions must be experienced vicariously through the priest. In the highly explicit book *Taboo: "The Ecstasy of Evil" (The Psychopathology of Sex and Religion)* (New Falcon Publications, 1991), we explore the *abnormalities* of such practices and the psycho-sociological phobic reactions to Sex Magic.

I do not intend to use this space to serve as an introduction to the theories or techniques of Sex Magic or Tantra.

There are many fine works available that introduce those subjects very well. For the reader who is already knowledgeable on these subjects, a few helpful hints concerning how Enochian can be used in these areas may prove valuable and rewarding.

The modern view that our normal waking consciousness stands somewhere between the limitless potential of transcendental experience and the "demons" that run amok in our subconscious mind is not too dissimilar to the medieval view that Mankind is sandwiched between God and the Angels, between Heaven and Hell. The working hypothesis of the magician of old went something like this, "God has dominion over me and compels me to do His will. I have dominion over the spirit world, (especially over the so-called fallen angels), and just as I look up to God, they look up to me, therefore, I can compel them to do my bidding."

In 1458, the noted Qabalist and court magician, Abraham the Jew, in his classic work, *The Book of the Sacred Magick of Abra-Melin The Mage*, took this concept of the hierarchy of responsibility a sublime step forward and catapulted magick to the same level as the Yogic disciplines.

Simply put, to work the magick, you must first be united with Divinity. (This experience he calls The Knowledge and Conversation of the Holy Guardian Angel.) This initiatory landmark is only accomplished after a six month period of purification and a strict regimen of ever-increasing longing for union with the Angel. Once this "marriage" is consummated and the "blessing" of the Angel's presence is bestowed, the magician immediately turns to the lower spiritual world and bestows the same "blessing" on the resident denizens and extracts from them a pledge of loyalty and support.

These wild and infernal spirits who, up until now were unacknowledged, uncontrolled and most likely at odds with the True Will of the magician, were now going to be given the opportunity to work for his and their greater good. And now that the magician had formed an intimate alliance with the Divine, he had the spiritual "authority" to force the lower spirits to cooperate.

Thus, Abraham the Jew reveals an indispensable truth: Magick demands an assault on two fronts at once. It requires realization of your responsibility not only to that which is above but also to that which is below.

It is only through *you* that the Divine (your Superconsciousness) can manifest on this plane. Without *you* the spirits of the Infernal regions (your subconsciousness) have no hope of "salvation" (balance and control). Indeed, without your controlling influence they will become a very real threat to your life and sanity. You must see to it that each area receives proper and equal attention. Neglect your higher aspiration and you will find that you soon lack the spiritual integrity to command the spirits. Neglect the spirits and they will sooner or latter surface to demand your attention. Wild beasts can be domesticated and trained to serve you. If you treat them well and allow them to share in your continuing good fortune they can realize their greater potentiality. However, if you abuse them or forget to feed them they will inevitably seize the first opportunity to break out and devour you for their needed nourishment.

The two pillars of the Enochian system, as outlined in *Liber Chanokh* are:
THE ELEMENTAL WATCH TOWERS OF THE UNIVERSE
AND THE TABLET OF UNION
THE WORLD OF THE ELEMENTAL BEINGS

THE THIRTY ÆTHYRS WHOSE DOMINION EXTENDETH
IN EVER-WIDENING CIRCLES WITHOUT AND BEYOND
THE WATCHTOWERS OF THE UNIVERSE.
THE WORLD OF THE DIVINE BEINGS

Both these worlds can be explored sexually and can provide the diligent magician with the joy and fulfillment of his or her Divine Beloved and the passion and energy of being the Divine Beloved to an Elemental lover.

Please pay close attention to the following.

ENOCHIAN SEX MAGIC
But to love me is better than all things.
Liber AL, I, 61

I will now proceed to ignore my own advice regarding other magician's visions. I hope the reader will recognize the value of what follows and will kindly forgive me.

In the series of visions of the 30 Æthyrs that Crowley chronicled in his remarkable work, *The Vision And The Voice*, he describes his vision of the Body of the great Goddess. The imagery is so powerful and his narrative colored with expressions of such tender awe, that one cannot but share, however temporarily, his overwhelming desire to unite with Her. To lose oneself utterly in Her would most certainly result in such intensity of bliss as to make the ecstasy of orgasm seem as a candle help up to the sun.

But that was Crowley's vision...Crowley's Great Goddess. To dwell on Her when you have your own Great Goddess (or God) "waiting" for your devotion would be as stupid as refusing a date with a lovely girl next door (who has secretly loved you all her life) because you have to sit at home alone, and pine over a painting of Helen of Troy.

Do you see where I'm heading with this? By a serious and concerted effort on your part, it is possible for you to achieve the highest level of spiritual experience your evolutionary-initiatory status will permit, including a relationship with the Divine Beloved. *Once you "know" Her (or Him) all subsequent "earthly" ecstasies take the form of devotional offerings to the Great Lover who rewards the devotee with increasingly sweeter embraces until finally the embrace is eternal.*

Where do you seek the initial Vision?

In yourself.

How can you start to look in yourself?

One way is by systematically skrying the 30 Æthyrs.

Nor let the fools mistake love; for there are love and love. There is the dove, and there is the serpent. Choose ye well!.

Liber AL, I, 57

In *The Little Mermaid*, Hans Christian Andersen writes of an Undine who is so enamored of a mortal man that she relinquishes her status as an immortal being for the opportunity to love and be loved by him. This charming tale contains a profound magical truth. Elemental spirits, whose natures are so specialized that they lack the balance of qualities necessary for sentient life, do indeed long for union with "complete" beings such as ourselves. Because their natures are universal they truly are immortal and if they should ever achieve union with a mortal they would actually "die" to their old, incomplete existence to be "born" into the life of their beloved. This is exactly what we do in our relationship with the Divine Principal.

The spirits of the Elemental Tablets are particularly suitable for such operations and all that is required is to call them up. It is so simple that you may set to work ill-prepared for success. A few words of caution might be in order.

Think before you proceed. Just what are you really prepared to handle? Experience has shown that it is most often wisest to contact a spirit from very low in the elemental hierarchy for operations such as this. Also, as in the everyday world, it is unwise to try to juggle too many of these relationships at the same time. If you think "Hell hath no fury like that of a *woman* scorned," think again. And sometimes jealousy *really is a green-eyed monster*.

Finally, and most importantly, *Never confuse your love for the Divine with your love for the Elemental*. The sexual "role" the magician assumes when making love to the Goddess (or God) is diametrically different than the "role" he or she plays when mating with an elemental spirit. In the former, the magician's attitude is that of adoration and awe and release is a gift from above, the result of ecstatic surrender. (To assume that attitude with an elemental lover would be spiritual suicide.) The sexual "role" the magician assumes with the elemental is one of loving dominance. The Spirit surrenders to you. You bestow your ecstasy as a gift and allow your elemental partner to share, through you, the Divine love.

Confusing these two "loves" is surely the fountainhead of all the ills sexual repression has visited upon mankind. If it is your Will to be a sex magician, see to it that you use your magick to face and conquer your life, not to hide from it.

Chapter Seven

Techniques Of Enochian Sex Magick
By Christopher S. Hyatt, Ph.D.

There is no evidence that the communicating Angels that delivered the Enochian system to Dr. John Dee and Edward Kelly ever instructed them concerning sexual applications of the art.

Biographers will be quick to point out the famous incident of April 1587 when, according to Kelly, the Angel Madimi suggested to Kelly that he and Dr. Dee share their wives in common. (Dee was absent during this communication). Enochian scholars argue that the text of this communication contains many flaws that do not characterize other less personal communications and that this may have been a case of magical wishful thinking on Kelly's part. Nevertheless it seems they did indeed swap wives and in spite of obvious attempts to erase the manuscript, the record confirms this. It seems the only "magical" result of this "operation" was the break up of Dee and Kelly as magical partners and the close of one of the most remarkable chapters in magical history.

To those knowledgeable in the theory and techniques of Tantra the keys of the Enochian system open a treasure-house of practical applications.

The exercises outlined below should be practised only after you have a thorough mastery of the system in all its non-sexual applications. Any uncertainties on the part of the magician as to what he or she is doing will destroy needed concentration and create a "break" which will absorb the entire force of operation. (In sexual workings that could be an overabundant amount of energy particularly if you perform the exercises in my Tantra book.)

EXPLORATION OF THE THIRTY ÆTHYRS

As written earlier in the text, the Thirty AEthyrs are the "heavens" or Aires of the system. Starting with the 30th AEthyr and working to the 1st, the Magician explores only as far as his or her personal level of Initiation will permit. This process is comparable to "pathworkings" of the Qabalistic system. In Enochian terms, the "Great Work" of the magician is to master all 30 AEthyrs. (Starting with 30 and ending with 1) experiences with the 30 AEthyrs are highly personal and entirely unique to each magician. Working with the AEthyrs can be a lifetime endeavor and it is entirely presumptuous and inappropriate for another individual to "guide" another in this area.

This personal aspect of the Æthyrs coupled with the simplicity of it's "one-Call-does-it" procedure makes it ideal for preliminary workings.

The great stumbling block to exploring the Æthyrs is the difficulty one encounters in "breaking through" to the next Æthyr. In the higher levels this may be because the magician has reached his or her initiatory limit. But in the lower Æthyrs it is more often the case that the magician simply can't "let go" and refocus his or her attention to the section of the brain where the vision is taking place. In Secrets of Western Tantra I provide an entire array of exercises which will help the Magician "let go."

The following exercise is intended exclusively for workings of the Thirty Æthyrs. There are two participants whom we will refer to as the Magician and the Assistant. For our illustration the male participant is the Magician and will recite the Call and "receive" the vision, the female participant is the Assistant and will eventually record the vision.

These gender roles are for illustration only. The Magician can just as easily be female and the Assistant male. This particular operation is equally effective for participants of the same sex and can also be adapted for solitary workings. *It makes absolutely no difference who is Magician and who is Assistant.* It is only important that a couple decide before the operation commences.

Note: There must be no ambiguity about the willingness of either participant to take part in an operation of this kind. If one participant has to be coerced, begged or tricked into participation the vortex of ill-will that will emanate from the offended party will insure not only the failure of the operation but also the destruction of a more precious "magical asset", the respect of another human being.

EXAMPLE:

The Magician wishes to explore the 30th Æthyr, **TEX**, and the Assistant has expressed to him that it is her Will to participate in the operation.

Both participants bathe and dress at first in simple, soft, white garments. You may light incense, burn candles or use lights or soft music to enhance the mood. Small amounts of alcohol are also useful.

Prepare the room in which you are working with the appropriate symbols for the Æthyr such as the sigils of the Governors or the Elemental Tablet from which they are taken. In the case of **TEX** it would be the Water Tablet. (One couple I know has the Elemental Tablets and the Tablet of Union constructed entirely of wooden pyramids which they painstakingly have painted and lettered in Enochian. These are placed on the floor, under their bed, prior to Æthyric or elemental workings.)

Begin by performing the Lesser Banishing Ritual of the Pentagram in the area in which you will be working. *(The student is referred to Appendix III for additional instructions.)*

THE LESSER BANISHING RITUAL OF THE PENTAGRAM

The Qabalistic Cross facing East:
Touch your Forehead and say **Atoh (aah-toh)**
Touch your Heart and say **Malkuth (mal-kooth)**
Touch your Right Shoulder and say **Ve-Geburah (veh-ghee-boo-rah)**
Touch your Left Shoulder and say **Ve-Gedulah (veg-ghee-doo-lah)**
Touch your Heart and say **Le-Olam (lee-oh-lum)**
Point the symbolic dagger inward and say **Amen (aah-mayn).**

Still facing East:
Trace the Banishing pentagram of Earth and vibrate **VHVH (yoad–hay–vaahv–hay)**, as you thrust your symbolic dagger into the heart of the pentagram.

With your arm still extended,
turn to the South:
Trace the Banishing pentagram of Earth and vibrate the name **ADONAI (Aah–doh–noy)**. {Remember to thrust the symbolic dagger as you vibrate each God name.}

With your arm still extended,
turn to the West:
Trace the Banishing pentagram of Earth and vibrate the name **EHIEH (eh–hayh–yah)**.

With your arm still extended,
turn to the North:
Trace the Banishing pentagram of Earth and vibrate the name **AGLA (ag–guh–lah)**.

With your arm still extended return to the East, completing the circle. Now Imagine yourself surrounded in a Flaming Circle of four Pentagrams.

Stand straight with your arms out forming the shape of a Cross:
Say:
Before me **Raphael (rah-fay-ale)**
Behind me **Gabriel (gaj-bree-ale)**
At my right shoulder, **Michael (mee-khigh-ale)**
At my left shoulder **Auriel (oh-ree-ale)**

Then Say:
Before me **flames the Pentagram**
Behind me **shines the six-rayed Star.**

Finish by repeating the Qabalistic Cross:

Touch your Forehead and say **Atoh**
Touch your Heart and say **Malkuth**
Touch your Right Shoulder and say **Ve-Geburah**
Touch your Left Shoulder and say **Ve-Gedulah**
Touch your Heart and say **Le-Olam**
Point the symbolic dagger inward and say **Amen.**

(See the Appendix for examples of the invoking and banishing Pentagrams of all the Elements which are used in Elemental Temple openings and invocations).

The Magician then recites the Call of the 30th Æthyr, **TEX**, (Madariatza das perifa **TEX**...etc.) while the Assistant simply relaxes and meditates upon the sounds of the Enochian Call.

When the Call is completed let the Magician slowly vibrate the names of the Governors. (In the case of **TEX** there are four Governors. All other Æthyrs have three.)

Then, (believe it or not), forget about the operation. Relax, take your time and enjoy each other's company. Build slowly and naturally to greater levels of arousal. Continue to do everything you can to sustain your love making (at least 25 minutes, but for God's sake don't keep looking at your watch!). The idea is to become joyfully and totally exhausted. Then at the moment of orgasm (and not a split second before) let the Magician remember the purpose of the operation (the Skrying of the Æther) and repeat the first line of the Call; **Madariatza das perifa TEX cahisa micaolazoda saanire caosago of fifsa balzodizodarasa Iaida**. This may be done verbally or mentally but it must be well memorized so that it can come forth effortlessly.

(Note: A tape recorder can be used for both repeating Calls and taking notes. Sometimes two recorders are very handy, one for taking notes and the other for playing Calls).

The Magician then falls exhausted and allows the flood of images to wash through his brain. The temptation to fall asleep will be almost irresistible and that is where the skill of the Assistant is most vital.

After a few quiet moments if the Magician is not relating his vision to the Assistant she must take it upon herself to question him. This requires a high degree of tact and subtlety for she does not want to disturb the vision and yet she cannot allow him to fall into a deeper state of unconsciousness. This takes practice. She should have a pad of paper and a pencil handy and should write down everything that the Magician says. She should be especially careful to correctly spell any unknown words or phrases and she should not hesitate to ask the Magician (or the entity speaking through the Magician) the correct spelling of Angelic words.

If the vision stalls and reaches a point where nothing further is happening the Assistant can sometimes give it a push.

EXAMPLE:

Magician: All I see is a bunch of trees. Nothing is happening.

Assistant: Try turning around. Do you see anything now?

Magician: Just more trees but there is a small pond in the middle.

Assistant: Walk over to the pond. Look in the pond and tell me what you see.

Magician: At first I see only my own reflection but as I keep looking I see that the pond is actually a bowl supported by the wings of four Angels, etc.

If angels or other beings appear in the vision they must be tested by repeating the names of the Governors one at a time. If the entity shows discomfort at the name of any of the Governors dismiss it by continuing to repeat the Governor's name until it disappears and a being appears that is strengthened by hearing the names.

Do not be afraid of anything you "see" or "hear". Maintain an attitude of good natured tolerance even if hideous sights or terrifying beings or creatures appear. Act like a dispassionate explorer. *Fear is failure and the forerunner of failure*.

When it is clear that the vision is finished, or when it is obvious that the Magician is now fatigued or ready to fall asleep it is time to end the operation.

It is of the utmost importance that the Magician now "snap out of it" for it is he who must banish and close the Temple. If the Magician is reluctant to "wake up" and perform his duties it is the Assistant's responsibility to *see that he does*. No effort should be spared to "break the spell" and return the Magician to the objective world. Turn on the lights, talk loudly, get a drink, or splash some water on your face.

Finally, he performs the Lesser Banishing Ritual of the Pentagram and the Magician and the Assistant review the notes and transfer them to the Magician's diary. The comments of the Assistant are often extremely important and should not be omitted in the record.

Often the couple will wish to change roles and explore the same Æthyr on a subsequent occasion. Allow at least one day between operations.

ELEMENTAL OPERATIONS AND CREATION OF THE MAGICKAL CHILD

Dr. Israel Regardie believed that certain sex magick techniques could be used by advanced students to incarnate "spiritual" energies on the physical plane, as well as making important shifts in the orientation of the Psyche and the Universe. In other words, if these methods were used properly, couples could bring into the world "divine" forces in the children they generated, who could influence the future of the race.

In addition to creating "real children" these methods could be used to create "bio-psycho-spiritual vessels", which would shift the focus of the mind as well as develop new powers and abilities.

The creation of the magickal child by ritualized sexual practices is symbolic in one sense of the whirling forces of nature, mixing and separating in their chaotic dance of creation.

This mixing and separating process is vividly displayed in the Elemental Tablets and the Tablet of Union of the Enochian system. Working with these basic forces of nature allows conscious co-operation and co-creating with the cosmos, and the magician becomes a miniature form of the cosmic process following its root law.

By willful and conscious co-operation the magician increases and refines his energies, sacrificing himself or herself willingly to Nature instead of being a passive food source in the spiritual food chain. The realization that man's emotional, physical and sexual energies are food for the "gods" can create great personal turmoil at first, however when one begins to joyously participate in the spiritual feeding frenzy, one is "elevated perpendicularly to infinity."

SELECTING THE MAGICKAL CHILD
THE ENOCHIAN METHOD

The selection process is the most difficult and, in truth, the most magickal, aspect of the operation. The "soul searching" necessary for such an important act is awesome and should not be embarked upon with a frivolous attitude.

The Enochian adept (and no other should embark upon such project) is intimately familiar with every area of the Elemental environment and with his or her current initiatory position relative to the Thirty Æthyrs. By reviewing his or her personal diaries of perhaps hundreds of non sexual Enochian workings, the Magician can determine the areas of the system that manifest the qualities which are desirable in the magickal child.

For the purpose of our illustration we will say that we wish create a magickal child of purity and beauty. A child capable of reflecting and transmitting energy and impressions without being affected. A child such as this might be a great actor or politician because in this child others see themselves reflected. This is charming and disarming to others because when they look at the child they will see only what they want to see.

By checking the records of our previous evocations we see that **TDIM**, the Kerub ruling the *Water* Subangle of *Water* is the perfect Spirit to manifest in such a child.

The technique as outlined below has been adapted from the exercise The Orgastic Circulation of Light and is an excellent example of Tantric Enochian evocation.

In Dr. Regardie's copy of Wilhelm's *Secret Of The Golden Flower*, 3rd impression, 1935, there are a number of passages underlined. Dr. Regardie was not a habitual underliner, thus we may assume that when he did underline it was for a very good reason. One of the passages which he underlined more than once contained references to the circulation of light.

In the next method, the proper circulation of light is essential for true magickal effects to occur and has been modified for use in creating the magickal child. It is urged that the partners should practice the ritual many times *prior* to including the sexual aspects. As a rule it is wise to practice this together holding hands or touching in some fashion.

At the time determined most auspicious for the conception of the magickal child the Temple is made ready, Banished, Cleansed and Consecrated.

The Temple is then opened in the Grade of the 3° = 8° as outlined in *Chanokh* and the two participants recite a brief Oath declaring their intention to perform this creative act.

PART I
THE GREAT WHIRLINGS

The male should be on his back and the female should sit on top of him. Move only when instructed unless the penis begins to lose its stiffness.

Begin by imagining a *scintillating white light* about the size of a small basketball forming above the head and piercing the top of the skull. This is called the Kether point. Now vibrate the Three Holy Names of God (from the Water Tablet). **MPH ARSL GAIOL** as the sphere of Light grows brighter and more energetic. Do this for five minutes.

On the last six vibrations of **MPH ARSL GAIOL** the female should move on each sound of the Names.

As the force of this whirling ball of power becomes exceedingly real for you and your partner, allow the energy to descend slowly through the head. Allow it to rest in the throat or Da'ath point. Here imagine a *lavender color*. Vibrate the Name of the Great Elemental King of Water, **RAAGIOSL** until the energy becomes exceedingly real for you and your partner.

Again on the last six vibrations of **RAAGIOSL** the female should move six times.

Bring the energy down through the chest until it rests at the Heart of Tiphareth. Vibrate the Names of the six Seniors of the Water Tablet, **SAIINOV, SOAIZNT, LAOAZRP, LIGDISA, SLGAIOL, LSRAHPM**. The color of light should be *golden yellow* growing brighter and clearer as you vibrate each Name.

On the six last vibrations of the names of the Seniors the female should move six times.

Move the power through the diaphragm and abdominal region to the pelvis (Yesod), and vibrate the Divine Names of the Calvary Cross, Water of Water, **NELAPR, OMEBB** visualizing a sphere of *deep purple*.

Here on the last ten vibrations of **NELAPR** and **OMEBB** the male should move ten times very slowly.

Finally, allow the energy to descend through the legs until it formulates at Malkuth, the feet. Both participants vibrate the name of Kerub, the Name of their magickal child **TDIM** visualizing a *black* sphere.

The male should again move ten times quickly on the final vibrations of the Child's name.

Now, draw the energy up from the Black light of Malkuth changing colors as described above as it ascends to Kether. When the light reaches Kether concentrate on the White brilliance of this region.

When the light is at Kether and your movements are complete, meditate silently for a few moments and then begin the circulation of white light.

Note: At times Dr. Regardie ignored the different colors and the Spheres and simply used the white scintillating light of Kether for each of the points. However, he and I agree that the colored system is better suited for the practice of Sex Magick.

PART II
THE ORGASTIC CIRCULATION OF LIGHT
Circulate the energy of the White Light as follows:

Allow it to descend downward and outward via the left side of the body during every exhalation. When it reaches the left foot, transfer the energy over to the right foot and allow it to ascend the right side of the body on the inhalation. This should be done at least 10 times. The partners should move slowly in unison 10 times.

The second circulation of energy begins in Kether and travels down the front of the body on the exhalation and then up the back of the body on the inhalation. This should be done at least ten times as well. The partners should move slowly in unison ten times.

The third circulation, beginning with Kether follows down through the body on the exhalation until it reaches Malkuth. The energy is drawn up through the body to Kether on the inhalation. When it reaches the Crown, imagine it to discharge like water from a fountain, at the end of each inhalation. The fire and sparks of this scintillating fountaining go up and out through the Crown and then descend down and encompasses the body on the exhalation. After the final circulation has been completed and the fountaining maintained for a few movements, the couple should begin moving and breathing heavily as they surround themselves with sparkling light. The movements should then become spontaneous and at the moment of orgasm the light should be gathered and thrust beyond Sahasrara, toward the Chakra with No Name.

PART III
THE CRYSTALLIZATION OF THE LIGHT

The orgastic Light of the Chakra of No Name may be likened to the Philosopher's Stone, The Golden Flower, or the Lotus. It is a body of light created by the process of transmutation of spiritual-sexual energy and is the womb of the magickal child. This is an experiential realization, thus, the proof of the pudding is in the Doing and Creating.

The process of transmutation requires the proper balance and mixing of heat and cold, passive and active, and white and black. In a broader sense we are using tremendous active forces to create a non-active force. The nurturing we provide the womb-child through our practices creates a worthy resting place of deep silence for the aspirants involved in the creation process.

The circulating of orgastic light is no doubt one of the most beautiful secrets of the Great Work. As the light circulates again and again and your practices become more powerful and refined, a crystallization occurs and you begin to form the magickal child. Whether you choose it to be physical or spiritual or both, the creation of this spirit body allows you to have contact with the forces of the higher Spiritual Body. You have not only opened the doors of perception, but can now begin the process of real action in a way unknown to those who lack this initiation.

The Enochian Dictionary*

A

WORDS	PHONETIC	ENGLISH
Aaf	(Ah-ahff)	Amongst
Aai (AAo)	(Ah-ah-ee)	Amongst
Aaiom	(Ah-ah-ee-ohm)	Amongst us
Aala	(Ah-ah-lah)	Placed you
Abaivonin	(Ah-bah-ee-voh-nee-noo)	Stooping Dragon
Abila (Apila)	(Ah-bee-lah)	Liveth forever
Aboapri	(Ah-boh-ah-pay-ree)	Let them serve you
Abraassa	(Ah-brah-ah-ess-sah)	Provided
Abrang	(Ah-brah-noo-gee)	I have prepared
ACAM	(Ah-kahm)	7, 6, 9, 9
Adgt	(Ah-dah-gee-tay)	Can
Adna	(Ah-dah-nah)	Obedience
Adohi	(Ah-doh-hee)	Kingdom
Adoian	(Ah-doh-ee-ah-noo)	Face
Adphaht	(Ah-dah-pay-hah-tay)	Unspeakable
Adroch	(Ah-dah-ronk-hay)	Olive Mount
Adrpan	(Ah-dah-ra-pahn-noo)	Cast down
Af	(Ah-eff)	Nineteen
Affa	(Ah-eff-fah)	Empty
Ag	(Ah-gee)	None, No
Aglo	(Ah-gloh)	In Thy
Alar	(Ah-lahr)	Have set
Aldi	(Ah-el-dee)	Of gathering
Aldon	(Ah-el-doh-noo)	Gather up, Gird
Allar	(Ah-el-lahr)	Bind up
Am	(Ah-em)	Beginning
Amipzi	(Ah-mee-pay-zoad-ee)	I fastened
Amiram	(Ah-mee-rahm)	Yourselves
Amis	(Ah-meess)	End
Amma	(Ah-em-mah)	Cursed
Ananael	(Ah-nah-nah-el)	Secret Wisdom
Anetab	(Ah-nay-tahb)	In government
Angelard	(Ah-nu-gee-lahr-dah)	His Thoughts
Aoiveae	(Ah-oh-ee-vay-ah-ay)	Stars
Ar	(Ah-ray)	To Vanne

*From the *Complete Golden Dawn System of Magic* by Israel Regardie (Falcon Press, 1984).

WORDS	PHONETIC	ENGLISH
Ar	(Ah-ray)	That (in order)
(Ar) Tabas	(Tah-bahs)	That Govern
ARN	(Ah-rah-noo)	2nd Æthyr
As	(Ah-ess)	Was
ASP	(Ah-ess-pay)	21st Æthyr
Aspt	(Ah-ess-pay-tay)	Before
Ath	(Ah-tay-hay)	Works
Atraah	(Ah-tay-rah-ah)	Your Girdles
Audcal	(Ah-vah-dah-kahl)	Mercury
Avavco	(Ah-vah-vah-koh)	Thunders of increase
Avavox	(Ah-vah-vohx)	His pomp
Aviny	(Ah-vee-nee)	Millstones
Aziagier	(Ah-zoad-ee-ah-gee-ayr)	Harvest
Aziazor	(Ah-zoad-ee-ah-zoad-ohr)	Likeness
Azieh	(Ah-zoad-ee-ay)	Whose hands

B

Babage (n)	(Bah-bah-gay)	South
Babalon (d)	(Bah-bah-lohn)	Wicked (harlot)
Baeouib	(Bah-ay-oh-veeb)	Righteousness
BAG	(Bah-gee)	28th Æthyr
Baghie	(Bah-gee-hee-ay)	Fury
Bable (r)	(Bah-bay-lay)	For, Because, For Why?
Bahal	(Bah-bah-lah)	Cried loudly
Balit	(Bah-leet)	The Just
Balt (an)	(Bah-lay-tay)	Justice
Baltim	(Bah-lay-teem)	Extreme Justice
Baltoh	(Bah-lay-toh)	The Righteous
Baltoha	(Bah-lay-toh-hah)	For my own righteousness
Balye	(Bah-lee-ay)	Salt
Balzarg	(Bah-lay-zoad-ar-gee)	Stewards, Presidents
Bal-zizras	(Bah-lay Zoad-ee-zoad-rahs)	Judgement
Bams	(Bahm-ess)	Let them forget
Basgim	(Bahs-geem)	Day
Bazm (elo)	(BAh-zoad-em)	Mid-day
Bia (l)	(Bee-ah)	Voices
Biah	(Bee-ah)	Stand
Bien	(Bee-ay-nu)	My voice
Bigliad	(Beeg-lee-ah-dah)	In our comforter
Blans	(Blah-noo-ess)	Harboured

WORDS	PHONETIC	ENGLISH
Blior	(Blee-ohr)	Continual comforters
Bliora	(Blee-oh-rah)	Comfort
Bliorax	(Blee-oh-rahx)	Shall comfort
Bliors	(Blee-oh-ray-ess)	Our comfort
Bogpa	(Boh-gee-pah)	Reigneth
Bolp	(Boh-lah-pay)	Be thou
Booapis	(Boh-oh-pees)	Let her serve them
Bramg	(Bay-ray-mee-gee)	Are prepared
Bransg	(Bay-ray-ness-gee)	Guard
Brgow	(Bay-rah-goh-vah)	Sleep
Brin	(Bay-reen)	Have
Brint	(Bay-reen-tay)	Hast
Busd	(Boos-dah)	Glory
Busdir	(Boos-dee-ray)	Glory
Butmon	(Boot-tay-mohn)	His mouth hath opened
Butmoni	(Boot-tay-moh-nee)	Their mouths

C

C	(Kah)	Unto, with
Cab	(Kah-bay)	Rod
Cacacom	(Kah-kah-cohm)	Flourish
Cacocasp	(Kah-koh-cahs-pay)	Another while
Cafafm	(Kah-fah-fahm)	Their abiding
Calz	(Kah-lah-zoad)	The firmament
Cam(piao)	(Kah-em)	While
Camliax	(Kah-em-lee-ahx)	Spake
Canal	(Kah-nah-lah)	Workmen
Caosg (o)	(Kah-oh-ess-gee)	The Earth
Capimaon	(Kah-pee-mah-oh-nu)	Numbers of Time
Capimi-ali	(Kah-pee-mee ah-lee)	Successively
Carbaf	(Kah-ray-bahf)	Sink
Cars (Cors)	(Kah-resss)	Such
Casarm	(Kah-sah-raym)	To Whom
Casarman	(Kah-sah-ray-mah-nu)	Under whose
Casarmg	(Kah-sah-ray-em-gee)	To Whom
Ceph	(Kay-pay-hay)	Title of (z)
Chirlan	(Kah-hee-ray-lah-nu)	Rejoiceth
Chis (or Chris)	(Kah-hees)	Are
Chisdao	(Koh-hees-dah-oh)	Diamonds
Chiso	(Kah-hee-soh)	Shall be
CHR	(Kay-hay-ray)	20th Æthyr

WORDS	PHONETIC	ENGLISH
Cial	(Kee-ah-lah)	9, 9, 9, 6
Ciaosi	(Kee-ah-oh-see)	Terror
Cicle	(Kee-kah-lay)	Mysteries of Creation
Cla	(Kee-lah)	4, 5, 6.
Cnila	(Kee-nu-lah)	Blood
Caozior	(Koh-ah-zoad-ee-ohr)	Increase
Cocasb	(Koh-kah-see-bay)	Time
Colis	(Koh-lees)	Making
Collal	(Koh-lay-lahl)	Stones
Commah	(Kohm-mah)	Bindeth, trussed together
Como	(Koh-moh)	A window
Comselh	(Kohm-say-lay-hay)	A circle
Conisbra	(Koh-nees-bay-rah)	The work of man
Const	(Kohn-ess-tay)	Thunders
Cophan	(Koh-pay-hah-nu)	Lamentation
Cor	(Koh-ray)	Number
Coraxo	(Koh-rah-x-oh)	Thunders of judgement
Cordiziz	(Koh-ray-dee-zoad-ee-zoad)	Reasonable creatures of earth, men
Cormp	(Koh-ray-em-pay)	Numbered
Cormp	(Koh-ray-em-pay)	Hath yet numbered
Cormpt	(Koh-ray-em-pay-tay)	Be numbered
Crcrg	(Kah-ray-kah-ray-gee)	Until
Cri-mi	(Kah-ree mee)	Praises
Cro-od-zi	(Koh-roh oh-dah zoad-ee)	The 2nd Beginning
C-rp (crip)	(Kah Ar-pay)	But

D

D (Dial)	(Dah)	Third
Da	(Dah)	There
Damploz	(Dah-me-pay-loh-zoad)	Variety
DAOX	(Dah-oh-x)	5, 6, 7, 8
Darbs	(Dah-ray-bah-ess)	Obey
DARG	(Dah-ray-gee)	6, 7, 3, 9
Darr	(Dah-ray-ray)	Philosopher's Stone
Darsar	(Dah-ray-sahr)	Wherefore
Dax	(Dahx)	Loins
Dazis	(Dah-zoad-ees)	Their Heads
De	(Day)	Of
DEO	(Day-oh)	7th Æthyr
DES	(Day-ess)	26th Æthyr

WORDS	PHONETIC	ENGLISH
Diu	(Dee-vah)	Angle
Dlafor	(Dah-lah-foh-dah)	Sulphur
Dluga (Dlagar)	(Dah-loo-gah)	Giving
Dlugam	(Dah-loo-gahm)	Given
Dlugar	(Dah-loo -gahr)	Gave them
Do	(Doh)	In
Doalim	(Doh-ah-leem)	Sin
Dobix	(Doh-beex)	Fall
Dodpal	(Doh-dah-pah-el)	Let them vex
Dods	(Doh-dahs)	Vexing
Dodseh	(Doh-dah-say-hay)	Vexation
Dooain (or p)	(Doh-oh-ah-ee-noo)	His name
Don	(Doh-noo)	Title of letter E (r)
Dorpha	(Doh-ray-pay-hah)	Have looked about me
Dorphal	(Doh-ray-pay-hahl)	Looking with gladness
Dosig	(Doh-see-gee)	Night
Drilpi (a)	(Dah-ree-lah-pah)	Great
Drix	(Dah-ree-x)	Bring down
Droln	(Dah-roh-lah-noo)	Any
Ds	(Dah-ess)	Who, that or which
Du-i-b (Duiv)	(Doo-ee-bay)	Into the third angle
Drun	(Dah-roo-noo)	Title of letter

E

E	(Ay)	I
Eca	(Ay-kah)	Therefore
Ecron	(Ay-kah-roh-noo)	Praise
Ed-nas	(Ay-dah Nah-ess)	Receivers
Ef	(Ay-eff)	Visit us
Efafage	(Ay-fah-fah-gay)	Vials
El	(Ay-lah)	The same
Elzap	(Ay-lah-zoad-ah-pay)	Course
Em	(Ay-mee)	Nine
Emod	(Ay-moh-dah)	8, 7, 6, 3
Emetgis	(Ay-may-tay-gees)	Seal
Emna	(Ay-mee-nah)	Herein
Enay	(Ay-nah-ee)	The Lord
Eors	(Ay-oh-ray-ess)	Thousand
Eran	(Ay-rah-noo)	6332 (6322)
Erm	(Ay-ray-mee)	Ark
Es	(Ay-ess)	Fourth

WORDS	PHONETIC	ENGLISH
Esiasch	(Ay-see-ar-ess-cha)	Brothers
Ethamz	(Ay-tay-hah-me-zoad)	Are covered
Etharzi	(Ay-tay-hah-ray-zoad-ee)	Peace

F

WORDS	PHONETIC	ENGLISH
F (also EF)	(Eff)	Visit
Fa-a-ip	(Fah-ah ee-pay)	Your voices
Faboan	(Fah-boh-ah-noo)	Poison
Fafeh	(Fah-fay-hay)	Intent
Fafen	(Fah-fay-noo)	Your train
Fam	(Fah-mee)	Title of S
Faod	(Fah-oh-dah)	The Beginning
Faonts	(Fah-oh-nu-tay-ess)	Dwelling (verb)
Faorgt	(Fah-ohr-gee-tay)	Dwelling place
Fargt	(Fah-ray-gee-tay)	Their dwelling places
Farmz	(Fah-ray-mee-zoad)	Ye lifted up your voices
Faxs	(Fahx-ess)	7336
Fifalz	(Fee-fah-lah-zoad)	Weed out
Fifis	(Fee-fee-ess)	Execute

G

WORDS	PHONETIC	ENGLISH
G	(Gee)	(With)
GA	(Gah)	31
Gah	(Gah-hay)	Spirits
Gal	(Gah-lah)	Title of D
G-chis-ge	(Gee Kah-hee-ess gay)	Are not the
Ge	(Gee)	Is not
Ged	(Gay-dah)	Title of G
Ge-Iad	(Gay Ee-ah-dah)	Our Lord and Master
Geobofal	(Gay-oh-bah-fah-lah)	Great Work
Ger	(Gay-ray)	Title of Q
Gigipah	(Gee-gee-pah-hay)	Living Breath
Gisa	(Gee-sah)	Title of T
Givi	(Gee-vee)	Stronger
Gizyaz	(Gee-zoad-ee-ah-zoad)	Mighty Earthquakes
Gnay	(Gee-nah-ee)	Doth
Gnetaab	(Gee-nay-tah-ah-bay)	Your Governments
Gnonp	(Gee-noh-nu-pay)	I garnished
Gohe (or Goho)	(Goh-hay)	Saith
Gohia	(Goh-hee-ah)	We say
Gohol	(Goh-hoh-el)	Saying
Goholor	(Goh-hoh-lohr)	Lift up

WORDS	PHONETIC	ENGLISH
Gohulim	(Goh-hoo-leem)	It is said
Gohus	(Goh-hoos)	I say
Gon	(Goh-noo)	Title of I
Gono	(Goh-noh)	Faith
Gosao	(Goh-sah-oh)	Stranger
Graa	(Gee-rah-ah)	Moon
Graa	(Gee-rah-ah)	Marquises
Graph	(Gee-rah-pay-hay)	Title of E
Grosb	(Gee-roh-ess-bay)	Bitter Sting

H

Hami	(Hah-mee)	Creatures
Harg	(Hah-ray-gee)	Hath planted
Hoath	(Hoh-ah-tay-hay)	True Worshipper
Holdo	(Hoh-lah-doh)	Groaned aloud
Hol-q	(Hoh-lah Koh)	Measureth (ed)
Hom	(Hoh-mee)	Liveth
Homil	(Hoh-mee-el)	True Ages
Homin	(Hoh-mee-noo)	Age
Hubai	(Hoo-bah-ee)	Lanterns
Hubar	(Hoo-bah-ray)	Ever burning lamps
Hubard	(Hoo-bah-ray-dah)	Living lamps

I

I	(Ee)	Is
Iad	(Ee-ah-dah)	God
Iadnah	(Ee-ah-dah-nah-hay)	Knowledge
Iadnamad	(Ee-ah-dah-nah-mah-dah)	The undefiled knowledge
Iadpil	(Ee-ah-dah-pee-el)	Him
Iaiadix	(Ee-ah-ee-ah-deex)	Honour
Ia-ial	(Ee-ah ee-ah-el)	Conclude us
Iaida	(Ee-ah-ee-dah)	The highest, most high
Iaidon	(Ee-ah-oee-doh-noo)	All-power
Ial	(Ee-ah-el)	Burning
Ialpirgah	(Ee-ah-el-pee-ray-gah)	Flames of first glory
Ialpon	(Ee-ah-el-poh-noo)	Burn
Ialpor	(Ee-ah-el-poh-ray)	Flaming
Iaod (of)	(Ee-ah-oh-dah)	Beginning
Iarry	(Ee-oh-ray-ree)	Providence
ICH	(Ee-kah-hay)	11th Æthyr

WORDS	PHONETIC	ENGLISH
Id	(Ee-dah)	Always
Idoigo	(Ed-doh-ee-goh)	Him that Sitteth on the Holy Throne
Ieh	(Ee-ay-hay)	Art
Iehusoz	(Ee-ay-hoo-soh-zoad)	His mercies
Iisonon	(Ee-ee-soh-noh-noo)	Branches
Ils	(Ee-el-ess)	O Thou
Ilsi	(Ee-el-see)	Thee
Im-va-mar	(Ee-mee vah mah-ray)	Apply yourselves
Insi	(Ee-noo-see)	Walkest
Iod	(Ee-oh-dah)	Him
Ioiad	(Ee-oh-ee-oh-dah)	Him that liveth forever
Ip	(Ee-pay)	Not
Ipam	(Ee-pah-mee)	Beginningless
Ipamis	(Ee-pah-mees)	Endless
Ipuran	(Ee-poo-rah-noo)	Shall not see
Yolcam	(Ee-oh-ol-kah-mee)	Bring forth
Yolci	(Ee-oh-el-kee)	Bringeth forth
Yor	(Ee-oh-ray)	Roll
Yrpoil	(Ee-ar-poh-ee-lah)	Division
Irgil	(Ee-ar-gee-lah)	How many
Isro	(Ee-ess-roh)	Promise
Ixomaxip	(Ee-x-oh-mohx-ee-pay)	Let her be known
Iza-zaz	(Ee-zoad-ah zoad-ah-zoad)	Have framed within
Izizio	(Ee-zoad-ee-zoad-oh-pay)	From the highest vessels

L

L	(Lah)	The first
L (o) (a)	(Lah)	The first one
Laiad	(Lah-ee-ah-dah)	The Secrets of Truth
Lap	(Lah-pay)	For
Larag	(Lah-rah-gee)	Neither
Las	(Lah-ess)	Rich
LEA	(Lah-ay-ah)	16th Æthyr
Lel	(Lay-lah)	The same
Levithmong	(Levee-tha-mon-gee)	The Beasts of the Field
LIL	(Lee-lah)	1st Æthyr
Limial	(Lee-em-lah-lah)	His Treasure
LIN	(Lee-noo)	22nd Æthyr
LIT	(Lee-tay)	5th Æthyr
LOE	(Loh-ay)	12th Æthyr

WORDS	PHONETIC	ENGLISH
Loholo (Sobolo)	(Loh-hoh-loh)	Shineth
Lolcis	(Loh-lah-kee-ess)	Bucklers
Loncho	(Loh-nu-kah-hoh)	Fall
Lon-doh	(Loh-noo doh)	Kingdoms
Lonse (Lonshi)	(Loh-noo-sah)	Power
Lonsh	(Loh-noo-ess-hay)	In power exalted
Lonshin	(Loh-noo-ess-hee-noo)	Their powers
Lors-l-q	(Loh-ray-ess el koh)	Flowers
Lrasd	(El-rah-ess-doh)	To dispose
Lring	(El-ree-nu-gee)	To stir up
Lu	(Loo)	Not or nor
Lucal	(Loo-kah-lah)	The North
Luciftian	(Loo-kee-eff-tee-ah-nu)	Ornaments of brightness
Luciftias	(Loo-ku-eff-tee-ah-ess)	Brightness
Lu-ia-he	(Loo ee-ah hay)	A Song of Honour
Lulo	(Loo-loh)	Tartar of Wine
Lusd (an)	(Loo-ess-dah)	Feet
Lusda	(Loo-ess-dah)	Their feet
Lusdi	(Loo-ess-dee)	My feet

M

Maasi	(Mah-ah-see)	Laid up
Mad	(Mah-dah)	The same your God
Madrid	(Mah-dah-ree-dah)	Iniquities
Madriiax	(Mad-dah-ree-ee-ahx)	O Ye Heavens
Malpirgi	(Mah-lah-pee-ar-gee)	Fires of life & increase
Malprg	(Mah-lah-pee-ar-gee)	Though-thrusting fire (Or Fiery Darts)
Mals	(Mah-lah-ess)	Title of P
Manin	(Mah-nu-nu)	In the Mind
Ma-of-fas	(Mah-ohff fahs)	Not to be measured
Mapm	(Mah-pay-mee)	9639
Marb	(Mah-ah-bay)	According
Matorb	(Mah-toh-ar-bay)	Echoing
MAZ	(Mah-zoad)	6th Æthyr
Med	(May-dah)	Title of O
Miam	(Mee-ah-mee)	Continuance
Mian	(Mee-ah-nu)	3663
Micalp	(Mee-kah-el-pay)	Mightier
Micalzo	(Mee-kah-el-zoad-oh)	In Power
Micaolz	(Mee-kah-oh-el-zoad)	Mighty
Micma	(Mee-kah-mah)	Behold

WORDS	PHONETIC	ENGLISH
Miinoag	(Mee-ee-noh-ah-gee)	Corners
Mir	(Mee-ray)	A torrent
Mirc	(Mee-ar-kah)	Upon
(z)Mnad	(Mee-nah-dah)	Another
Molap	(Moh-lah-pay)	Men
Molvi	(Moh-lah-vee)	Surges
Mom	(Moh-mee)	Moss
Momao	(Moh-mah-oh)	The Crowns
Momar	(Moh-mah-ray)	Shall be crowned
Monasci	(Moh-nah-ess-kee)	The Great Name
Monons	(Moh-noh-noo-ess)	Heart
Mooab	(Moh-oh-ah-bah)	It repenteth me
Mospleh	(Moh-ess-pay-lay-hay)	The Horns
Moz	(Moh-zoad)	Joy

N

WORDS	PHONETIC	ENGLISH
Na	(Nah)	Your
Na-hath	(Nah Hah-tay-hay)	Title of H
Nana-e-el	(Nah-nah ay ay-lah)	My Power
Nanba	(Nah-noo-bah)	Thorns
Napeai	(Nah-pah-ay-ee)	Oh you swords
Napta	(Nah-pah-tah)	Two edge sword
Nazarth	(Nah-zoad-ahth)	Pillars of gladness
Nazavabb	(Nah-zoad-ah-vah-bay-bay)	Hyacinthine Pillars
Nazps	(Nah-zoad-pay-ess)	Sword or Earls
Netaab	(Nay-tah-ah-bay)	Government
NI	(Nee)	28
NIA	(Nee-ah)	24th Æthyr
Nibm	(Nee-bah-mee)	Season
Nidali	(Nee-dah-lee)	Mighty Sounds
Niis	(Nee-ee-ess)	Come Ye
Niiso	(Nee-ee-soh)	Come Away
Noaln	(Noh-ah-lah-noo)	May (be)
Noan (Noas)	(Noh-ah-noo)	Ye are become
(i) Noar	(Noh-ah-ray)	Become
Noasmi	(Noh-ah-ess-mee)	Let them become
Nobloh	(Noh-bay-loh)	The Palms
Noco	(Noh-koh)	Servant
Nocod	(Noh-koh-dah)	Thy servants
Noib	(Noh-ee-bay)	Yea!
Nonig	(Noh-mee-gee)	Even
Nonca	(Noh-noo-kah)	Unto You

WORDS	PHONETIC	ENGLISH
Nonci (f)	(Noh-noo-kee)	O You (ye)
Noncp	(Noh-noo-kah-pay)	For You
Noquodi	(Noh-koo-oh-dee)	Their Ministers
(c) Noquol	(Noh-koo-oh-lah)	O Ye Servants
Nor	(Noh-ray)	Sons
Noromi	(Noh-roh-mee)	O Ye Sons!
Nor-molap	(Noh-ray moh-lah-pay)	Sons of Men
Nor-quasahi	(Noh-ray koo-ah-sah-hee)	Ye Sons of pleasure
Norz	(Noh-ray-zoad)	Six
Nothoa	(Noh-tay-hoh-ah)	In the midst (?)

O

O	(Oh)	5
O	(Oh)	Be
Oado	(Oh-ah-doh)	Weave
Oadriax	(Oh-ah-dah-ree-ahx)	Lower Heavens
Oali	(Oh-ah-lee)	I have placed
Oanio	(Oh-ah-nee-oh)	Moment
OB	(Oh-bay)	28
Obelisong	(Oh-bah-lee-soh-noo-gee)	Pleasant deliverers
Obloc	(Oh-bay-loh-kah)	A Garland
Oboleh	(Oh-boh-lay-hay)	Your Garments
Obza	(Oh-bay-zoad-ah)	Half
Od	(Oh-dah)	And
Odo	(Oh-doh)	Open or Openest
Odzi	(Oh-dah-zoad-ee)	Beginning
Oe	(Oh-ay)	Sing (ing)
O-q	(Oh koh)	But
Ohio	(Oh-hee-oh)	Woe
Ohorela	(Oh-ho-ray-lah)	I made a Law, Dukes
Oi	(Oh-ee)	This (or that is)
Oiad	(Oh-ee-ah-dah)	Just or God
Oiap	(Oh-ee-ah-pay)	The same
OL	(Oh-lah)	24th part
Ol	(Oh-lah)	I made you (I have made)
Olani	(Oh-lah-nee)	Two Times
Ollor	(Oh-lah-loh-ray)	Man
(Ollora, Ollog)	(Oh-lah-loh-rah)	Same
Oln	(Oh-lah-noo)	Made
Olpirt	(Oh-lah-pee-ray-tay)	Light

WORDS	PHONETIC	ENGLISH
Om	(Oh-mee)	Know or Understand
Omoas	(Oh-mah-ah-ess)	Their Names
Oma (p)	(Og-mah)	Understanding
Omax	(Oh-mahx)	Knowest
Ooa	(Oh-oh-ah)	Their
Ooaona	(Oh-oh-ah-oh-nah)	Eyes, visible appearance
Ooge	(Oh-oh-gay)	Chamber
Op	(Oh-pay)	22
Oroch (a)	(Oh-roh-kah-hay)	Under you (beneath)
Orri	(Oh-ray-ree)	Barren Stone
Ors	(Oh-ray-ess)	(with darkness)
Orscor	(Oh-ray-ess-koh-ray)	Dryness
Orsca	(Oh-ray-ess-kah)	Building
Orsha (Orsba)	(Oh-ray-ess-hah)	Drunken
Orth	(Oh-raytha)	Title of F
Os	(Oh-ess)	Twelve
Othil	(Oh-tay-hee-lah)	I have set
Ovcho	(Oh-voh-kah-hoh)	Let it confound
Ovof	(Oh-voh-eff)	May be magnified
Ovoars	(Oh-voh-ah-ar-ess)	The Center
Ox	(Ohx)	26
Oxex	(Ohx-ayx)	Vomit out
Oxiayal	(Ohx-ee-ah-yahl)	Mighty Seat
OXO	(Ohx-oh)	15th Æthyr
Ozazm	(Oh-zoad-ah-zoad-mee)	Make me
Ozol	(Oh-zoad-oh-lah)	Their heads
Ozongon	(Oh-zoad-oh-nu-goh-nu)	Manifold Winds
Ozozma	(Oh-zoad-oh-zoad-mah)	And make us

P

P	(Pay)	8
Pa	(Pah)	Be
Pa-aox (t)	(Pah-ahx)	Remain
Paeb	(Pah-ay-bay)	An Oak
Page	(Pah-gay)	Rest
Paid	(Pah-ee-dah)	Always
Pal	(Pah-lah)	Title of X
Pambt	(Pah-mee-bay-tay)	Unto me
Panpir	(Pah-noo-pee-ray)	Pouring down
Paombd	(Pah-oh-mee-bay-day)	Her members
Papnor	(Pah-pay-noh-ray)	This remembrance

WORDS	PHONETIC	ENGLISH
Par	(Pah-ray)	In Them
Parach	(Pah-rah-kah-hay)	Equal
Paracleda	(Pah-rah-kah-lay-dah)	A wedding
Paradial	(Pah-rah-dee-ah-lah)	Living dwellings
Paradizod	(Pah-rah-dee-zoad-oh-dah)	Virgins
Parm	(Pah-ray-mee)	Run
Parmg	(Pah-ray-mee-gee)	Let it run
Pashs	(Pah-ess-hay-ess)	Children
Patralx	(Pah-tay-rah-layx)	Rock
PAZ	(Pah-zoad)	4th Æthyr
Pd	(Pah-dah)	Thirty-three
Pe	(Pay)	Title of B
PEOAL	(Peh-oh-ah-lay)	5, 9, 6, 3, 6
Pi	(Pee)	Places (Bed)
Piad	(Pee-ah-dah)	Your God
Pi-adph	(Pee ah-dah-pay-hay)	Depths of my Jaws
Piamo-l	(Pee-ah-moh-ell)	Righteousness
Piap	(Pee-ah-pay)	Balance
Pidiai	(Pee-dee-ah-ee)	Marble
Pii	(Pee-ee)	Bed (or She is a place)
Piiah	(Pee-lah)	Moreover
Pild	(Pee-lah-dah)	Continually
Pilzin	(Pee-lah-zoad-ee-nu)	Firmament of Waters
Pir	(Pee-ray)	Holy Ones
Piripsax	(Pee-ree-pay-sahx)	With the Heavens
Piripsol	(Pee-ree-pay-sohl)	The Heavens
Plapli	(Pay-lah-pay-lee)	Partakers
Plosi	(Pay-loh-see)	As many
Poamal	(Poh-ah-mah-lah)	Your Palace
Poilp	(Poh-ee-lah-pay)	Are divided
Pop	(Poh-pay)	19th Æthyr
Praf	(Pay-rah-eff)	Dwell
Prdzar	(Pay-ray-dah-zoad-ahr)	Diminish
Prg	(Pay-ray-gee)	Flames
Prge	(Pay-ray-gay)	With the Fire
Prgel	(Pay-ray-gay-lah)	Of Fire
Priaz (i)	(Pay-ree-ah-zoad)	Those
Prt	(Pay-ray-tay)	Flame
Pugo	(Poo-goh)	Unto
Pu-im	(Poo-eem)	Sharp sickles (Knights)

WORDS	PHONETIC	ENGLISH
Q		
Q	(Koh)	Or
Q (Cocasb)	(Koh)	Content of Time
Qaa	(Kah-ah)	Your Garments
Qaaon (s)	(Kah-ah-oh-noo)	In Your Creation
Qanis	(Kah-nee-ess)	Olives
Qting	(Koh-tee-noo-gee)	The Rotten
Quaal (Quaadah)	(Koo-ah-ah-lah)	The Creator
Quar	(Koo-ah-ray)	1636
Quasb	(Koo-ah-ess-bay)	Destroy
Quasahi	(Koo-ah-sahee)	Pleasure
Qui-i-n	(Koo-ee ee noo)	Wherein
Qurist	(Koo-arel-ess-tay)	As an handmaid
R		
R	(Ar)	
Ra-as (y)	(Rah ah-ess)	The East
Raclir	(Rah-kah-lee-ray)	Weeping
Restel	(Ray-ess-tay-lah)	That you may praise Him
RII	(Ree-ee)	29th Æthyr
Rior	(Ree-or-rah)	Widow
Ripir	(Ree-pee-rah)	No place
Ripson	(Ree-pay-soh-noo)	Heaven
Rit	(Ree-tay)	Mercy
Rlodnr	(Ree-loh-dah-noo-ar)	Mercury
(Ror)	(Roh-ray)	Sun, Kings
Roxtan	(Rohx-tah-nu)	Wine
Rsam	(Rah-sah-em)	Admiration
S		
S	(Ess)	Fourth
Sa	(Sah)	In
Saanir	(Sah-ah-nee-ray)	Parts
Salbrox	(Sal-lah-brohx)	Sulphur
Sald	(Sah-lah-dah)	Wonder
Salman	(Sah-lah-mah-nu)	A house
Samvelg	(Sahm-vay-lah-gee)	To the Righteous
Sapah	(Sah-pah)	Mighty Sounds
Sision	(See-see-oh-noo)	Temple

WORDS	PHONETIC	ENGLISH
Siatris	(See-ah-tay-ree-ess)	Scorpions
Sibsi	(See-bay-see)	The Covenant
So	(Soh)	In
Sobam	(Soh-bah-mee)	Whom
Sobha	(Soh-bay-hah)	Whose
Sobra	(Soh-bay-rah)	In whose
Solpeth	(Soh-lah-pay-tay-hay)	Hearken
Sonuf	(Soh-noof)	Reign
Surzas	(Soo-ray-zoad-ah-ess)	He hath sworn
Symp	(See-mee-pay)	Another

T

T	(Tay)	Also
Ta	(Tah)	As
Taba	(Tah-bah)	To Govern
Tabaame	(Tah-bah-ah-may)	Prelates (governors)
Tabaan	(Tah-bah-ah-nu)	Governor
Tabaord	(Tah-bah-oh-ray-day)	Let her be governed
Tabaori	(Tah-bah-oh-ree)	Govern
Tabges	(Tah-bay-gay-ess)	Caves
Tal	(Tah-lah)	Title of M
Talbo	(Tah-lah-boh)	Cups
TAN	(Tah-noo)	17th Æthyr
Tastax	(Tah-ess-tayx)	Going Before
Tatan	(Tah-tah-noo)	Wormwood
Teloah	(Tay-loh-ah)	Death
Teloc (Vovim)	(Tay-loh-kah)	Him that is fallen
Teloch	(Tay-loh-kah-hay)	Death
TEX	(Tayx)	30th Æthyr
Thild	(Tay-hee-lah-dah)	Their own Seats
Thil (n)	(Tay-hee-lah)	Seats
Ti	(Tee)	It
Tia	(Tee-ah)	Unto us
Tianti	(Tee-ah-nu-tee)	She is (or bed)
Tibibf	(Tee-bee-bay-eff)	Sorrow
Tilb	(Tee-lah-bay)	Her
Tiobl	(Tee-oh-bay-lah)	In her
Tliob	(Tay-lee-oh-bay)	Separate, to
Toatar	(Toh-ah-tay-ray)	Hearken
Toh	(Toh-hay)	Triumpheth
Toglo	(Toh-gee-loh)	All things

WORDS	PHONETIC	ENGLISH
Toibl	(Toh-ee-bay-lah)	Within her
Tonug	(Toh-nu-gee)	Let them be defaced
Tooart	(Toh-oh-oh-ray-tay)	Furnishing
TOR	(Toh-ray)	23rd Æthyr
Torg (i)	(Toh-ray-gee)	Creatures of Earth
Torzu	(Tor-zoad-oo)	Arise
Torzul	(Toh-ray-zoad-oo-lah)	Shall Rise
Torzulp	(Toh-ray-zoad-oo-lah-pay)	Rose Up
Tox	(Tohx)	Of Him
Tranan	(Tay-rah-noh-noo)	Marrow
Trian	(Tay-ray-ee-ah-nu)	Shall Be
Trint	(Tay-ray-ee-nu-tay)	Sit
Trof	(Tay-roh-eff)	Building
Turbs	(Toor-bay-ess)	Their Beauty

V

Vabzir	(Vah-bay-zoad-ee-ray)	Eagle
Vaoan	(Vay-oh-ah-noo)	Truth (purified, glorified)
Vau	(Vah-oo)	Title of U or V
Vaul	(Vah-oo-lah)	Work
Vaun	(Vah-oo-nu)	Ye might work
Veim	(Vah-kah-ee-mee)	They frown not
Veh	(Vay-hay)	Title of C or K
Vap	(Vay-pay)	Flame
Vgear	(Vah-gay-ah-ray)	The strength of man
Vgeg (i)	(Vah-gay-gee)	Wax Strong
Vi	(Vee)	In
Vi-i-v	(Vee-ee-vah)	The second angle
Vin	(Vee-noo)	Invoke
Virq	(Vee-ray-koh)	Nests
Vi-v	(Vee vah)	The Second
Vlcinin	(Vah-lah-kee-nee-nu)	Happy is He
Vls	(Vah-lah-ess)	The Ends
V-ma-dea	(Vah-mah-day-ah)	Strong Towers
Vmd	(Veh-mee-dah)	Called
Vml	(Vah-mee-lah)	Add
Vmplif	(Vah-mee-pay-lee-eff)	Our Strength
Vnalah	(Vah-nah-lah)	Skirts
Vnas (Vnal)	(Vah-nah-ess)	These
Vnchi	(Vah-noo-kah-hee)	Confound

WORDS	PHONETIC	ENGLISH
Vnd-l	(Vah-noo-dah-lah)	The rest
Vnig	(Vah-nee-gee)	Requireth
Vniglag	(Vah-nee-gee-lah-gee)	Descend
Vnph	(Von-pay-hay)	Anger
Vohim	(Voh-hee-mee)	Hundred
Vonpho	(Von-pay-hoh)	Wrath
Vonsarg	(Voh-nu-sah-ray-gee)	Everyone
Vooan	(Voo-ah-nu)	Truth, with them that fall
Vorsg	(Vor-sah-gee)	Over You
Vovina	(Voh-vee-nah)	The Dragon
Vp	(Vah-pay)	Not
V-pa-ah (i)	(Vah pay ah-hay)	Wings
Vran	(Vah-rah-noo)	The Elders
Vrbs	(Vah-ray-bay-ess)	Beautified
Vrelp	(Vah-ray-lah-pay)	A Strong Seer of Things
VTA	(Vah-tah)	14th Æthyr
VTI	(Vah-tee)	25th Æthyr
VX	(Vah-ex)	42
Un	(Oo-noo)	Title of A
Ur	(Oo-ray)	Title of L
Uran	(Oo-rah-noo)	Shall see

Z

Z (od)	(Zoad)	They (as)
ZAA	(Zoad-ah-ah)	27th Æthyr
Zacar-e	(Zoad-ah-kah-ray)	Move
Zamran	(Zoad-ah-mer-rah-noo)	Show Yourselves
Zar	(Zoad-ah-ray)	(Courses)
ZEN	(Zoad-ay-noo)	18th Æthyr
ZID	(Zoad-ee-dah)	8th Æthyr
Zien	(Zoad-ee-ay-nu)	My hands
Zildar	(Zoad-ee-lah-dah-ray)	Flew
Zilodarp	(Zoad-ee-loh-dah-ray-pay)	Conquest
ZIM	(Zoad-ee-mee)	13th Æthyr
Zimii	(Zoad-ee-mee-ee)	Have entered
Zimz (a)	(Zoad-ee-mee-zoad)	My vestures
ZIP	(Zoad-ee-pay)	9th Æthyr
Zir	(Zoad-ee-ray)	I am
Zirdo	(Zoad-ee-ray-doh)	I am

Zirn	(Zoad-ee-ray-noo)	Wonders
Zirom	(Zoad-ee-roh-mee)	There were
Zirop	(Zoad-ee-roh-pay)	Was
Zixlay	(Zoad-ix-lay)	To stir up
Zizop	(Zoad-ee-zoad-oh-pay)	Vessels
Zilda	(Zoad-lee-dah)	To water
Znrza	(Zoad-nu-ray-zoad-ah)	Sware
Z-ol	(Zoad oh-lah)	Hands
ZOM	(Zoad-oh-mee)	3rd Æthyr
Zomd	(Zoad-oh-mee-dah)	In the midst of
Zonac	(Zoad-oh-nah-kah)	They are apparelled
Zongon	(Zoad-oh-nu-goh-nu)	The Winds
Zonrensg	(Zoad-on-raynu-ess-gee)	Delivered
Zorge	(Zoad-or-gee)	Be friendly unto me
Zumbi	(Zoad-oo-mee-bee)	Seas
Zylna	(Zoad-ee-lah-nah)	In itself

Appendix I
PART I

The Enochian Calls (Keys)

As we have seen, Crowley could be breathtakingly economical with his use of words as he almost nonchalantly elucidates upon rather intricate technical matters. In Part II of *Liber Chanokh*, he explains in eight rather complex sentences how the 19 Calls of the system are used to activate and access the spiritual forces of the Tablet of Union and the Elemental Tablets. The reader may find the table that follows an even more user friendly key to this process than the one I've outline in the text.

CALL	ELEMENTAL TABLET	CALL USED FOR...
1	TABLET OF UNION	...is used *first* in all invocations of Angels of the Tablet of Union. According to the Golden Dawn it is never used for actions dealing with angels of the Elemental Tablets.
2	TABLET OF UNION	...is used *second* (after Call 1) to invoke Angel EHNB of Tablet of Union. According to the Golden Dawn it is never used with Elemental Tablets.
3	TABLET OF AIR	...can be used in one of three ways: 1) used *third* (after Calls 1 and 2) to invoke Angels of EXARP of the Tablet of Union, or... 2) used *first* for operations involving Elemental Tablet of Air, or... 3) used *by itself* for invocations of the Planetary Seniors from the Elemental Tablet of Air; or for angels from the Air Subangle of the Elemental Tablet of Air.

CALL	ELEMENTAL TABLET	CALL USED FOR...
4	TABLET OF WATER	1) used *third* (after Calls 1 and 2) to invoke Angels of HCOMA of Tablet of Union, or... 2) used *first* for operations involving the Elemental Tablet of Water, or... 3) used *by itself* for invocations of the Planetary Seniors from the Elemental Tablet of Water, or for Angels from the Water Subangle of the Elemental Tablet of Water.
5	TABLET OF EARTH	...can be used in one of three ways: 1) used *third* (after Calls 1 and 2) to invoke Angels of NANTA of Tablet of Union, or... 2) used *first* for operations involving the Elemental Tablet of Earth, or... 3) used *by itself* for invocations of the Planetary Seniors from the Elemental Tablet of Earth, or for Angels from the Earth Subangle of the Elemental Tablet of Earth.
6	TABLET OF FIRE	...can be used in one of three ways: 1) used *third* (after Calls 1 and 2) to invoke Angels of BITOM of Tablet of Union, or... 2) used *first* for operations involving the Elemental Tablet of Fire, or... 3) used *by itself* for invocations of the Planetary Seniors from the Elemental Tablet of Fire, or for Angels from the Fire Subangle of the Elemental Tablet of Fire.
7	TABLET OF AIR	...used *after Call 3* to call forth or visit the Angels of the Water Subangle of the Elemental Tablet of Air.

CALL	ELEMENTAL TABLET	CALL USED FOR...
8	TABLET OF AIR	...used *after Call 3* to call forth or visit the Angels of the Earth Subangle of the Elemental Tablet of Air.
9	TABLET OF AIR	...used *after Call 3* to call forth or visit the Angels of the Fire Subangle of the Elemental Tablet of Air.
10	TABLET OF WATER	...used *after Call 4* to call forth or visit the Angels of the Air Subangle of the Elemental Tablet of Water.
11	TABLET OF WATER	...used *after Call 4* to call forth or visit the Angels of the Earth Subangle of the Elemental Tablet of Water.
12	TABLET OF WATER	...used *after Call 4* to call forth or visit the Angels of the Fire Subangle of the Elemental Tablet of Water.
13	TABLET OF EARTH	...used *after Call 5* to call forth or visit the Angels of the Air Subangle of the Elemental Tablet of Earth.
14	TABLET OF EARTH	...used after *Call 5* to call forth or visit the Angels of the Water Subangle of the Elemental Tablet of Earth.
15	TABLET OF EARTH	...used *after Call 5* to call forth or visit the Angels of the Fire Subangle of the Elemental Tablet of Earth.
16	TABLET OF FIRE	...used *after Call 6* to call forth or visit the Angels of the Air Subangle of the Elemental Tablet of Fire.
17	TABLET OF FIRE	...used *after Call 6* to call forth or visit the Angels of the Water Subangle of the Elemental Tablet of Fire.
18	TABLET OF FIRE	...used *after Call 6* to call forth or visit the Angels of the Earth Subangle of the Elemental Tablet of Fire.

PART I

An Alternate Pronunciation of The Calls (Keys)

The version of the Calls that Crowley presents us in *Liber Chanokh* follows rather closely the Golden Dawn's preference of adding a vowel sound after each consonant in the words. For instance: the first words of the First Call which when rendered letter-for-letter from the Angelic language to English would be:
"Ol sonf vorsg, gohó Iad balt…"
is altered to be pronounced:
"Ol sonuf vaoresaji, gohu IAD Balata…"
This gives an almost Italian lilt to the language and, arguably, helps it roll off the tongue in a more attractive manner. It is, however, something that was not suggested in the original Dee and Kelly material; indeed, there were even instances in which the communicating Angels cautioned against additions to the sounds indicated by the individual letters.

Be that as it may, I originally learned the Crowley/Golden Dawn pronunciation method and used it with success for years. As I mentioned earlier, I believe the angelic intelligences, *like the French*, appreciate any attempt to speak their language.

Today, however, I use a pronunciation method I feel is more consistent with the pronunciation guide originally delivered to Dee and Kelly. It was developed by the great linguist, the late Dr. Donald C. Laycock.[7] Below is a version of the Calls I have compiled from Dr. Laycock's material and my researches into the original Dee and Kelly material.

The First Call

Ol sonf vorsg, gohó Iad balt lansh calz vonpho, sobra z-ol ror i ta nazpsad Graa ta Malprg Ds hol-q Qa-a nothóa zimz, Od commah ta nobloh zien: Soba thil gnonp prge aldi Ds urbs óbôleh

---

[7] Laycock, Donald. *The Complete Enochian Dictionary: A Dictionary of the Angelic Language As Revealed to Dr. John Dee and Edward Kelly* (York Beach, ME: Weiser Books, 2001).

grsam: Casarm ohoréla cabá pir Ds zonrensg cab erm Iadnah. Pïlah farzm od znrza adna od gono Iädpil Ds hom od tóh, Soba Iaod Ipam Ul Ipâmis, Ds lóhôlo vep zomd Poamal od bogpa aäi ta piap piamos od vaoan: ZACARe c-a od ZAMRAM: odo cicle Qaa: zorge, lap zirdo noco MAD: Hoath Iaida.

I reign over you, sayeth the God of Justice, in power exalted above the firmaments of wrath: in whose hands the Sun is as a sword and the Moon as a through-thrusting fire which measureth your garments in the midst of my vestures, and trussed you together as the palms of my hands: Whose seats I garnished with the fire of gathering and (which) beautified your garments with admiration: to whom I made a law to govern the holy ones and delivered you a rod with the ark of knowledge. Moreover you lifted up your voices and swear obedience and faith to him that liveth and triumpheth whose beginning is not, nor end can not be, which shineth as a flame in the midst of your palace and reignneth amongst you as the balance of righteousness and truth. Move, therefore, and show yourselves: open the Mysteries of your Creation: Be friendly unto me: for I am the servant of the same your God, the true worshipper of the Highest.

The Second Call

Adgt v-pa-âh zongom fa-á-ip sald viv L sobam Iál-prg I-zâ-zaz pi-ádph, Cas-arma abramg ta talho paráclêda Q-ta lors-l-q turbs öoge Baltoh. Giui chis Lusd orri. Od micalp chís bia ózôngon. Lap noán trof cors ta ge, o-q manin Ia-í-don. Torzu góhel. ZACAR ca c-nó-qod: ZAMRAN micalzo: Od ozazm vrelp Lap zir Ioiad.

Can the wings of the winds understand your voices of wonder O you the second of the first, whom the burning flames have framed within the depth of my Jaws, whom I have prepared as Cups for a wedding, or as the flowers in their beauty for the Chamber of righteousness. Stronger are your feet than the barren stone. And mightier are your voices than the manifold winds. For you are become a building such as is not, but in the mind of the All powerful. Arise, sayeth the First. Move therefore unto his Servants: Show yourselves in power: And make me a strong Seer: for I am of him that liveth forever.

The Third Call

Micma gohó Piad zir cómselh azien biab Os Lón-doh. Norz chis óthil Gigîpah, und-l chis tá pû-im: Q mos-pleh teloch Qui-i-n toltorg chis I-chis-ge, m ozíen dst brgda od torzul í-lí E ól balzarg od áâla Thiln os ne-tâ-ab dluga vomsarg Lonsa cap-mi-áli vors cla homil cocasb, fafen izízop od miinôag de gne-táab vaun na-ná-ê-el: panpir Malpirgi caósg Pild noan unalah balt od vooán. do-ó-i-ap MAD Gohólor gohús amiran. Micma Iehúsoz ca-cá-com od do-o-â-in noar mi-cá-olz a-aí-om. Casármg gohia: ZACAR, unîglag od Im-uâ-mar pugo plapli anánael Qáan.

Behold, sayeth your god, I am a Circle on whose hands stand 12 Kingdoms. Six are the seats of Living Breath, the rest are as sharp sickles: or the horns of death wherein the Creatures of ye earth are to are not, except mine own hand which sleep and shall rise In the first I made you Stewards and placed you in seats 12 of government, giving unto every one of you power successively over 456, the true ages of time, to the intent that from your highest vessels and the corners of your governments you might work my power: powering down the fires of life and increase continually on the earth Thus you are become the skirts of Justice and Truth. In the Name of the same your God, lift up, I say, your selves. Behold his mercies flourish and Name is become mighty amongst us. In whom we say: Move, Descend and apply your selves unto us, as unto the partakers of the Secret Wisdom of your Creation.

The Fourth Call

Othíl lasdi babâge od dorpha Gohól G-chisge avávâgo Cormp pd dsonf viv-di-v Casármi Oali Mapm Sobam ag cormpó c-rp-l Casarmg croódzi chis od vgeg dst capimáli chis Capimaon lonshin chis ta Lo Cla: Torgú Nor quasáhi, od F caósaga: Bagle Zirenáiad, Dsi od Apâla. Do-ó-â-ip Q-á-al ZACAR, od ZAMRAN Obelisong rest-el aaf Nor-mô-lap.

I have set my feet in the south and have looked about me, saying, are not the Thunders of increase numbered 33 which reign in the Second Angle under whom I have placed 9639 Whom none hath yet numbered but one, in whom the second beginning of things are and wax strong, which also successively are the number of time: and their powers are as the first 456: Arise, you Sons of pleasure, and visit the earth: for I am the Lord your God, which is, and liveth. In the name of the Creator, Move and show yourselves as pleasant deliverers that you may praise him amongst the sons of men.

The Fifth Call

Sapáh zímii du-i-v od noas ta-qa-a-nis adroch dorphal Ca ósg od faonts péripsol tablior Casarm amipzi nazarth af od dlugar zizop z-lida caósgi toltórgi od z-chis esîasch L taviu od iaád thild ds peral hubar Peóal soba cormfa chis ta la vls od Q-có-casb. Ca niis od Darbs Q-á-as, Feth-ar-zi od blióra. ia-ial ed-nas cicles: Bágle? Geiad i L.

The mighty sounds have entered into the third Angle and are become as olives in the olive mount, looking with gladness upon the earth and dwelling in the brightness of the heavens as continual comforters, unto whom I fastened pillars of gladness 19 and gave them vessels to water the earth with her creatures and they are the brothers of the first and second and the beginning of their own seats which are garnished with continually burning lamps 69636 whose numbers are as the first, the ends and the contents of time. Therefore come you and obey your creation, visit us in peace and comfort. Conclude us as receivers of your mysteries: for why? Our Lord and Master is all One.

The Sixth Call

Gah s díu chis em micálzo pilzin sobam El harg mir babálon od obloc samvelg dlugar malprg arcaósgi od Acám canal sobólzar f-bliard caosgi od chis anétab od miam ta viv od d. Darsar solpeth bien: Brita od zácam g-micálzo, sob-há-hath trían Lu-iá he odecrin MAD Q-a-a on.

The spirits of the 4th Angle are Nine, Mighty in the firmament of waters: whom the first hath planted a torment to the wicked and a garland to the righteous giving unto them fiery darts to vanne the earth and 7699 continual Workmen whose courses visit with comfort the earth and are in government and continuance as the second and the third. Wherefore hearken unto my voice: I have talked of you and I move you in power and presence, whose Works shall be a song of honor and the praise of your God in your Creation.

The Seventh Call

Raas isâlman paradiz oécrîmi aao ial-pîrgah qui-in enay butmon od inóas ni paradîal casarmg vgéar chirlan od zonac Luciftian cors to vaul zirn tol-hâ-mi Soba Londóh od miam chis tad o dés vmadêa od piblîar Othílrit od miám. Cnoquol Rit, ZACAR, ZAMRAN, oëcrimi Q-a-dah: od omicaolz aaîom Bagle papnor idlúgam lonshi od vmplif vgêgi Biglîad.

The East is a house of virgins singing praises amongst the flames of first glory wherein the Lord hath opened his mouth and they are become 28 living dwellings in whom the strength of man rejoiceth, and they are appareled with ornaments of brightness such as work wonders on all creatures. Whose Kingdoms and continuance are as the third and fourth strong towers and places of comfort, The seats of mercy and continuance. O you Servants of Mercy, Move, Appear, sing praises unto the Creator and be mighty amongst us. For to this remembrance is given power and our strength waxeth strong in our Comforter.

The Eighth Call

Bazmêlo i ta pirípson oln Nazâvábh ox casarmg vrán chis vgeg dsa-bramg baltôha gohó î-ad soba miam trian ta lól-cis Abaíuônin od aziágîer rior. Irgil chís da ds pá-â-ox busd Caósgo ds chis odípûran téloâh cacrg O isâlman loncho od Vouéna carbaf. Niíso, Bagle aváuâgo gohón: Niíso, bagle mómâo siáîon od mábza Iad-oiás-mômar poilp. Niis ZAMRAN ciaofi caósgo od bliors od corsi ta a-brâmig.

The Midday the first is as the third heaven made of Hyacinth Pillars 26 in whom the Elders are become strong which I have prepared for my own righteousness sayeth the Lord whose long continuance shall be as bucklers to the stooping Dragons and like unto the harvest of a Widow. How many are there which remain in the glory of the earth, which are, and shall not see death until this house fall and the Dragon sink? Come away, for the Thunders have spoken: Come away, for the Crowns of the Temple and the coat of him that is, was, and shall be crowned are divided Come, Appear to the terror of the earth and to our comfort and of such as are prepared.

The Ninth Call

Mi-ca-ôli bransg prgel napta ialpor (ds brin efáfâfe P vonpho oláni od obza: sobca vpâah chis tatan od tranan balye) alar lusda sobôln od chís hôlq Cnoquódi cial. vnál aldon mom caósgo ta las óllor gnay limlal: Amma chiis sobca madrid zchis, oöanôan chiis auíny drilpi caósgin od od butmôni parm zumvi Cníla: Daziz ethámz a-chíldao od mirc ózól chis pidiai collal vlcínin a-sóbam vcim. Bagle? Iadbáltoh chirlan par Niiso od ip ofafâfe Bagle acósasb icórsca vnig blior.

A mighty guard of fire with two-edged swords flaming (which have vials 8 of wrath for two times and a half: whose wings are of wormwood and of the marrow of salt) have settled their feet in the West and are measured with their Ministers 9996. These gather up the moss of the earth as the rich man doth his treasure: Cursed are they whose iniquities they are, in their eyes are millstones greater then the earth, and from their mouths run seas of blood: their heads are covered with diamond, and upon their hands are marble sleeves. Happy is he on whom they frown not. For why? The God of righteousness rejoiceth in them! Come away, and not your Vials, for the time is such as requireth comfort.

The Tenth Call

Coráxo chis cormp od blans Lucal azíâzor pæb, Soba Lilônon chis virq op eôphan od
Raclir maâsi bagle caosgi, ds ialpon dosig od basgim: od oxex dazís siâtris od salbrox cynixir fabôan Vnâl-chis coust ds dâox cocasg ol oánîo yor eors vóhim ol gizyax od math cocasg plosi molui ds pagêip Larag om droln matorb cocasb emna. L patralx yolci math nomig monons olôra gnay angêlard Ohio Ohio Ohio Ohio Ohio Ohio noib Ohio Caósgon Bagle madrid I, ziróp, chiso drilpa. Niiso crip ip nidâli.

The Thunders of Judgment and Wrath are numbered and are harbored in the North in the likeness of an oak, whose branches are Nests 22 of lamentation and weeping laid up for the earth, which burn night and day: and vomit out the heads of scorpions and live sulfur mingled with poison. These be The Thunders that 5678 times in the 24th part of a moment roar with a hundred mighty earthquakes and a thousand times as many surges. which rest not neither know any echoing time here. One rock bringeth forth 1000, even as the heart of man doth his thoughts. Woe, Woe, Woe, Woe, Woe, Woe, yea Woe be to the earth! For her iniquities is, was and shall be great. Come away: but not your noises.

The Eleventh Call

Oxiayal holdo od zirom O coráxo ds zildar raâsy, od vabzir comlîax od báhal, Niiso. salman telóch Ca-sár-man hol-q od ti ta z-chis soba cormf i ga. Niisa. Bagle abramg noncp. ZACARe ca od ZAMRAN. odo cicle qaá. Zorge lap zirdo noco Mad, Hoath Iaida.

The Mighty Seat groaned and they were 5 thunders which flew into the East, and the Eagle spake and cried with a loud voice, Come away. and they gathered themselves together in the house of death of whom it is measured and it is as they are, whose number is 31. Come away. For I have prepared for you. Move therefore, and show your selves. open the Mysteries of your Creation. be friendly unto me: for I am the servant of the same your God, the true worshipper of the Highest.

The Fifteenth Call
Ils tabâan Liálprt casarman vpaáhi chis darg dsoâdo caôsgi orscor ds ômax monasci Bæôuib od emetgis iaíâdix. ZACAR od ZAMRAN, odo cicle Qäa, zorge, Lap zirdo noco MAD, hoath Iaïda.

O Thou the governor of the first flame under whose wings are 6739 which weave the earth with dryness which knowest of the great name Righteousness and the Seal of Honor. Move and show your selves, open the Mysteries of your Creation, be friendly unto me, for I am the servant of the same your God, the true worshipper of the Highest.

The Sixteenth Call
Ils viuíâlprt salman blat ds acroódzi busd od bliôrax balit, dsinsi caosg lusdan Emod dsom od tliob drilpa geh yls Madzilodarp. ZACAR od ZAMRAN, odo cicle Qöa, zorge, Lap zirdo noco MAD, hoath Iaída.

O Thou second flame the house of Justice which hast thy beginning in glory and shalt comfort the just, which walkest on the earth with feet 8763 that understand and separate creatures, great art Thou in the God of Stretch Forth and Conquer. Move and show your selves, open the Mysteries of your Creation, be friendly unto me, for I am the servant of the same your God, the true worshipper of the Highest.

The Seventeenth Call
Ils dialprt soba vpâah chis nanba zixlay dodsih, od brint Faxs hubaro tustax ylsi, sobaíad I vónpôvnph, Aldon daxil od toátar. ZACAR od ZAMRAN, odo cicle Qäa, zorge, Lap zirdo Noco MAD hoath Iaïda.

O Thou third flame whose wings are thorns to stir up vexation, and hast 7336 lamps living going before thee, whose God is Wrath in Anger, gird up thy loins and harken. Move and show yourselves, open the Mysteries of your Creation, be friendly unto me, for I am the servant of the same your God, the true worshipper of the Highest.

The Twelfth Call

Nonci dsonf Babage od chis ob, hubíâo tibibp, allar atraâh od ef. drix fafen Mian ar E nay ovof soba dooâin aai i VONPH. ZACAR, gohus, od ZAMRAM, odo cicle Qaa. Zorge, Lap zirdo noco MAD, Hoath Iaida.

O you that reign in the South and are 28, the lanterns of sorrow, bind up your girdles and visit us. Bring down your train 3663 that the Lord may be magnified whose name amongst you is Wrath. Move, I say, and show yourselves, open the Mysteries of your Creation. be friendly unto me, for I am the servant of the same your God, the true worshipper of the Highest.

The Thirteenth Call

Napêai Babâgen dsbrin vx ooáôna lring vonph doâlim, eôlis ollog orsba ds chis affa. Micma isro MAD od Lon-shi-tox ds ivmd aai GROSB. ZACAR od ZAMRAN. odo cicle Qäa, Zorge, Lap zirdo Noco MAD, Hoath Iaïda.

O you swords of the South which have 42 eyes to stir up the wrath of sin, making men drunken which are empty. Behold the promise of God and his power which is called amongst you a Bitter Sting. Move and show your selves. open the Mysteries of your Creation: be friendly unto me: for I am the servant of ye same your God, the true worshipper of the Highest.

The Fourteenth Call

Norómi bagíe pasbs oîad ds trint mirc ol thil dods tolham caósgo Homin, ds brin oroch Quar, Micma bial oîad aîsro tox dsivm aai Baltim. ZACAR od ZAMRAN. odo cicle Qäa. Zorge, Lap zirdo Noco MAD, hoath Iaïda.

O you sons of fury, the daughters of the Just, which sit upon 24 seats vexing all creatures of the earth with age, which have under you 1636, behold the Voice of God promise of him which is called amongst you Fury or Extreme Justice. Move and show your selves. open the Mysteries of your Creation. be friendly unto me. For I am the servant of the same your God, the true worshiper of the Highest.

The Eighteenth Call

Ils Micaólz Olprit ialprg Bliors ds odo Busdir oîad ouôars caósgo, Casarmg Laíad erán brints casâsam, ds ivmd á-q-lo adóhi MOZ od maóffas, Bolp comobliort pambt. ZACAR od ZAMRAN, odo cicle Qäa, zorge, Lap zirdo Noco MAD, hoath Iaïda.

O Thou mighty Light and burning flame of comfort which openest the glory of God to the center of the earth, in whom the Secrets of Truth 6332 have their abiding, which is called in thy kingdom JOY and not to be measured, be Thou a window of comfort unto me. Move and show your selves, open the Mysteries of your Creation, be friendly unto me: for I am the servant of the same your God, the true worshipper of the Highest.

The Call of the Thirty Æthyrs

The Nineteenth Call is used to open each of the 30 Æthyrs. Only the name of the Æthyr itself (the third word in the first sentence) is changed.

Each Æthyr (with the exception of the 30th) is inhabited by three Governors who could be considered personifications of the nature of the Æthyr. I believe that after the Call has been recited, and before settling down to scry, it is important to pronounce, vibrate, or otherwise incorporate the names of the Governors in a brief invocation.

The names of the Æthyrs and their Governors are listed on the next page in Figure 90. If you wish to incorporate the sigils of the Governors (the Symmetrical Characters) for visualizations or to create talismans they can be found in chapter Nineteen in column VI of Figure 63.

The Nineteenth Call

Madriax dspraf [Name of Æyther, e.g. TEX or RII or BAG] chis Micaólz saánir Caósgo, od físis balzizras Iaída, nonca gohúlim, Micma adoían MAD, Iáod bliorb, sabaooáôna chis Lucíftîas

Figure 90. Legend: Æthyr/Governor Table

1			11			21		
LIL	1	Occodon	ICH	31	Molpand	ASP	61	Chirspa
	2	Pascomb		32	Vsnarda		62	Toantom
	3	Valgars		33	Ponodol		63	Vixpalg
2	4	Doagnis	**12**	34	Tapamal	**22**	64	Ozidaia
ARN	5	Pacasna	LOE	35	Gedoons	LIN	65	PARAOAN
	6	Dialiua		36	Ambriol		66	Calzirg
3	7	Samapha	**13**	37	Gecaond	**23**	67	Ronoamb
ZOM	8	Virooli	ZIM	38	Laparin	TOR	68	Onizimp
	9	Andispi		39	Docepax		69	Zaxanin
4	10	Thotanp	**14**	40	Tedoond	**24**	70	Orcanir
PAZ	11	Axziarg	VTA	41	Viuipos	NIA	71	Chialps
	12	Pothnir		42	Ooanamb		72	Soageel
5	13	Lazdixi	**15**	43	Tahando	**25**	73	Mirzind
LIT	14	Nocamal	OXO	44	Nociabi	UTI	74	Obuaors
	15	Tiarpax		45	Tastoxo		75	Ranglam
6	16	Saxtomp	**16**	46	Cucarpt	**26**	76	Pophand
MAZ	17	Vauaamp	LEA	47	Lauacon	DES	77	Nigrana
	18	Zirzird		48	Sochial		78	Bazchim
7	19	Opmacas	**17**	49	Sigmorf	**27**	79	Saziami
DEO	20	Genadol	TAN	50	Aydropt	ZAA	80	Mathula
	21	Aspiaon		51	Tocarzi		81	Orpamb
8	22	Zamfres	**18**	52	Nabaomi	**28**	82	Labnixp
ZID	23	Todnaon	ZEN	53	Zafasai	BAG	83	Focisni
	24	Pristac		54	Yalpamb		84	Oxlopar
9	25	Oddiorg	**19**	55	Torzoxi	**29**	85	Vastrim
ZIP	26	Cralpir	POP	56	Abaiond	RII	86	Odraxti
	27	Doanzin		57	Omagrap		87	Gomziam
10	28	LEXARPH	**20**	58	Zildron	**30**	88	Taoagla
ZAX	29	COMANAN	CHR	59	Parziba	TEX	89	Gemnimb
	30	TABITOM		60	Totocan		90	Advorpt
							91	Dozinal

perípsol, ds abraássa noncf netááib Caósgi od tilb adphaht dámploz, toóat noncf gmicálzôma Lrásd tófglo marb yárry IDOIGO od torzulp iáodaf gohól, Caósga tabaord saánir od christéós yrpóil tióbl, Busdir tilb noaln paid orsba od dodrmni zylna. Elzáptilb parmgi perípsax, od ta qurlst booapiS. Lnibm ovcho symp, od Christéos Agtoltorn mirc Q tióbl Lel. Ton paombd dilzmo aspian, Od christêos ag L tortorn parach asymp, Cordziz dodpal od fifalz Lsmnad, od fargt bams omaóas, Conísbra od auâuox tonug, Orscatbl noâsmi tabges Levithmong, unchi omptilb ors. Bagle? Moóóah ol córdziz. L capîmao ixomaxip od cacócasb gsâa. Baglen pii tianta abábâlond, od faórgt telocvovim. Mádrîiax torzu oádriax orócha abóâpri. Tabâóri priáz artabas. Adrpan corsta dobix. Yolcam priazi arcoazior. Od quasb qting. Ripir paaoxt sagácor. vml od prd-zar cácrg Aoivéâe cormpt. TORZV, ZACAR, od ZAMRAN aspt sibsi butmôna ds surzas tia baltan. ODO cicle Qáa, od ozama plapli Iadnâmad.

O you heavens which dwell in the First Æyther are mighty in the parts of the Earth, and execute the Judgment of the Highest, to you it is said, Behold the face of your God, the beginning of comfort, whose eyes are the brightness of the heavens, which provided you for the government of the Earth and her unspeakable variety, furnishing you with a power understand to dispose all things according to the providence of Him that sitteth on the Holy Throne, and rose up in the beginning saying: the Earth let her be governed by her parts and let there be division in her, that the glory of her may be always drunken and vexed in it self. Her course, let it run with the heavens, and as a handmaid let her serve them. One season let it confound an other, and let there be no creature upon or within her the same, All her members let them differ in their qualities, and let there be no one creature equal with an other: the reasonable Creatures of the Earth let them vex and weed out one an other, and the dwelling places let them forget their names: the work of man, and his pomp, let them be defaced: his buildings let them become caves for the beasts of the field. Confound her understanding with darkness. For why? It repenteth me I made Man. One while let her be known and an other while a stranger: because she is the bed of a Harlot, and the dwelling place of Him that is Fallen. O you heavens arise: the lower heavens underneath you, let them serve you! Govern those that govern: cast down such as fall! Bring forth with those that increase, and destroy the rotten! No place let it remain in one number: add and diminish until the stars be numbered! Arise, Move, and Appear before the Covenant of his mouth, which he hath sworn unto us in his Justice. Open the Mysteries of your Creation: and make us partakers of Undefiled Knowledge.

APPENDIX II
The Enochian Diagrams

The Corrected Holy Table
Diagram A

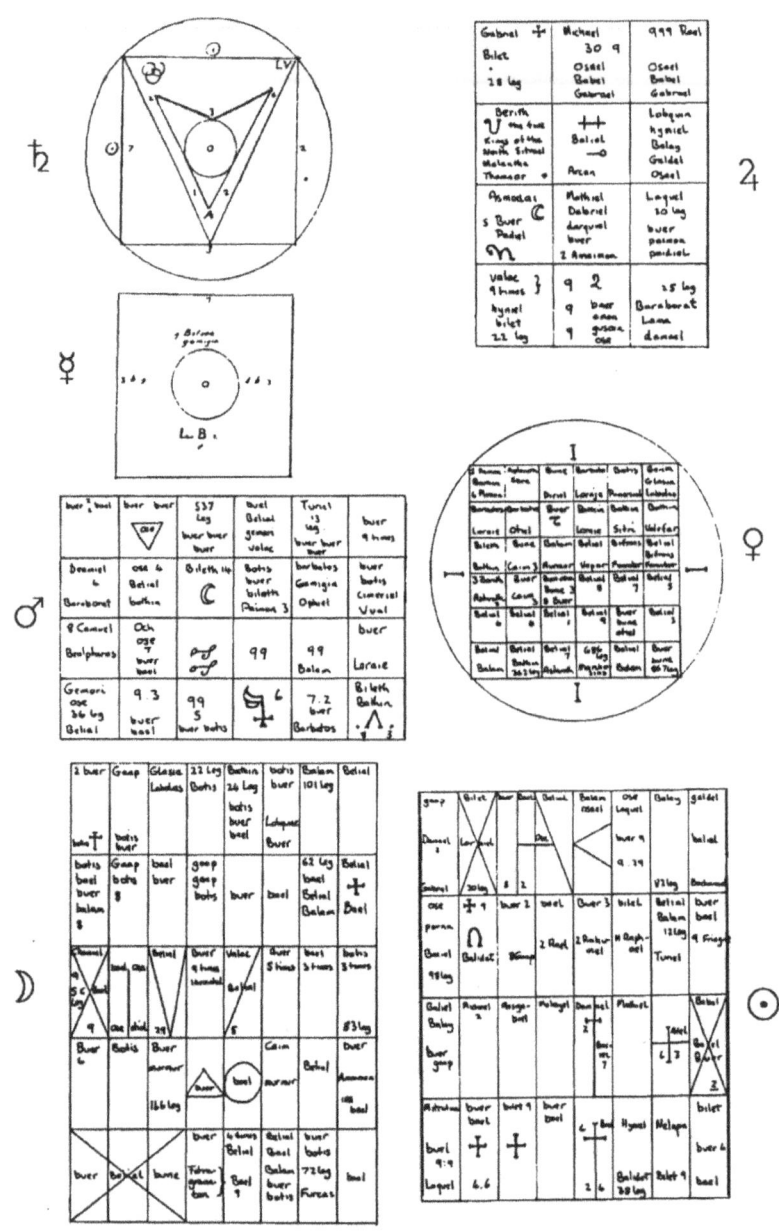

**Planetary Talismans
Diagram B**

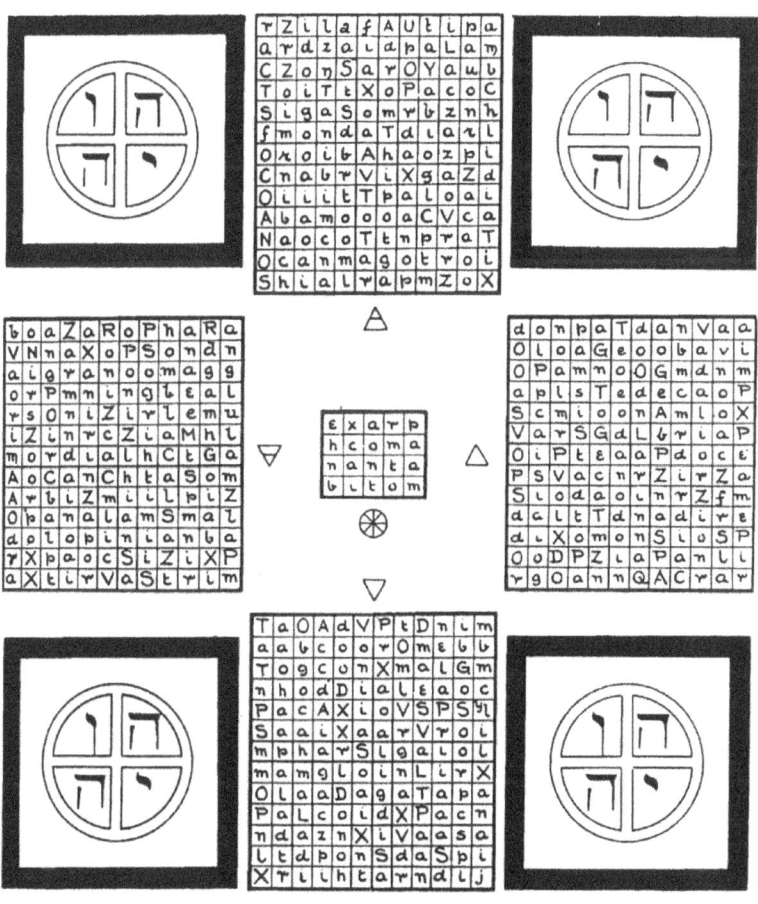

**The Elemental Tablets And Cherubic Emblems
Diagram C**

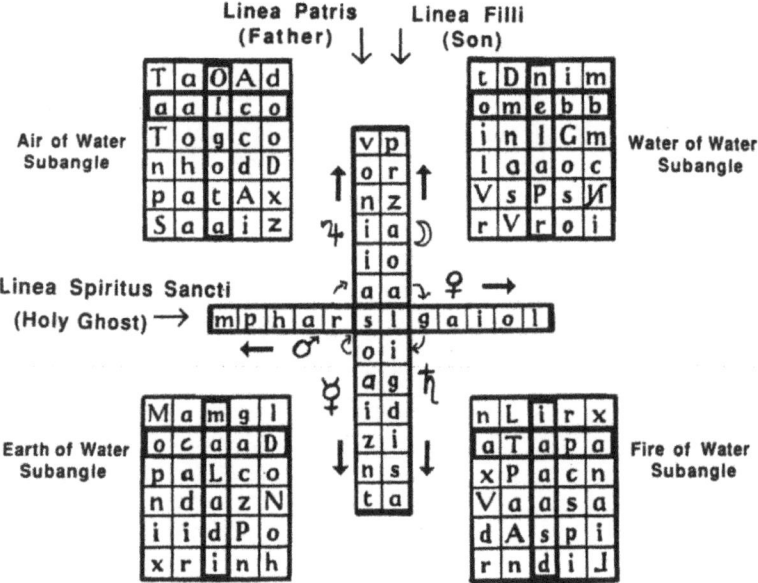

The Tablet of Water
Great Central Cross And Subangles
Diagram D

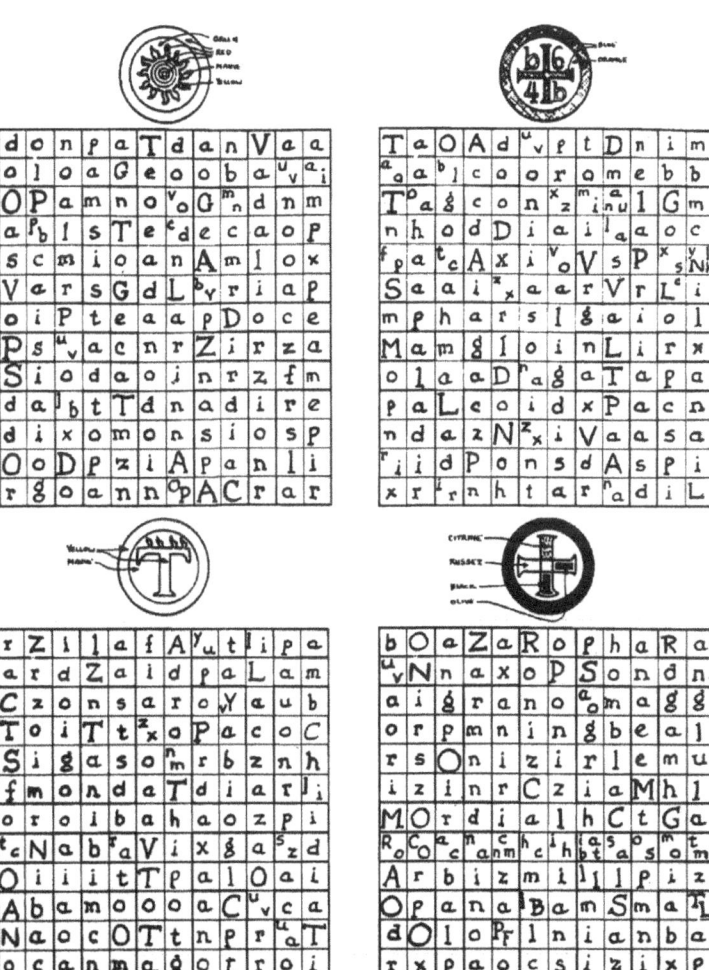

**Four Elemental Tablets With Alternate Spellings
Diagram E**

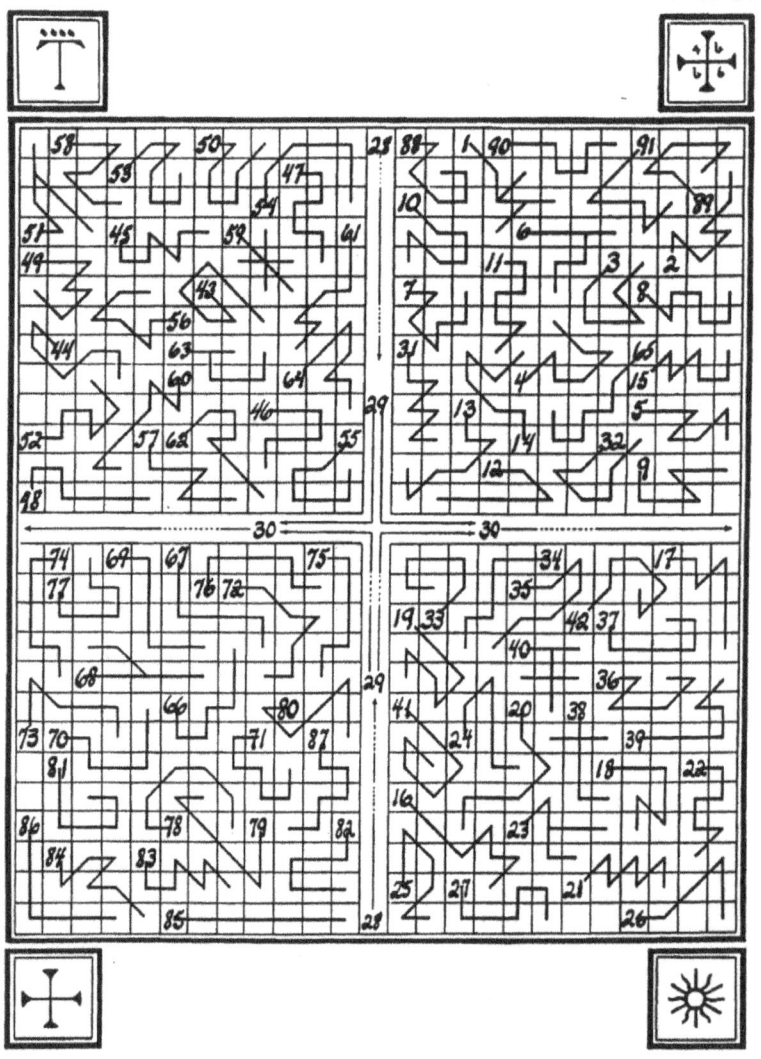

The Sigils Of The Governors
Diagram F

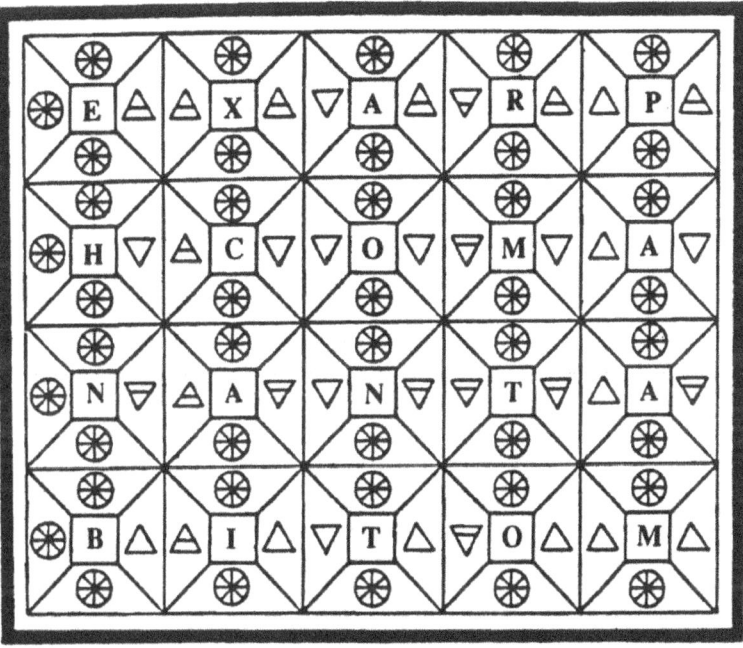

The Tablet of Union (English Letters)
Diagram G

Pentagrams Diagram H

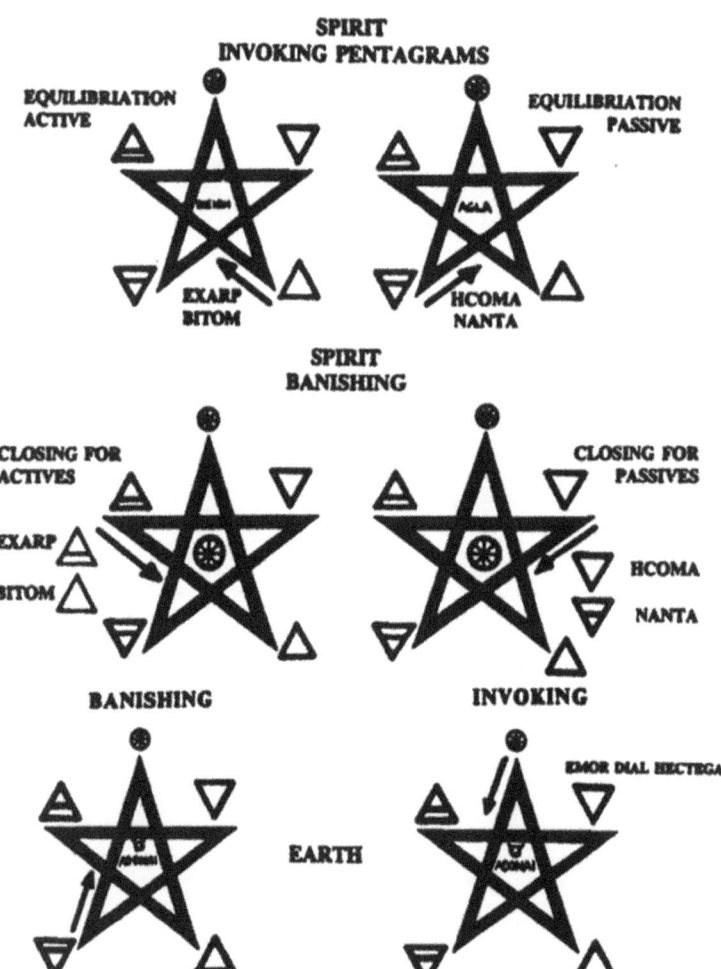

Pentagrams continued

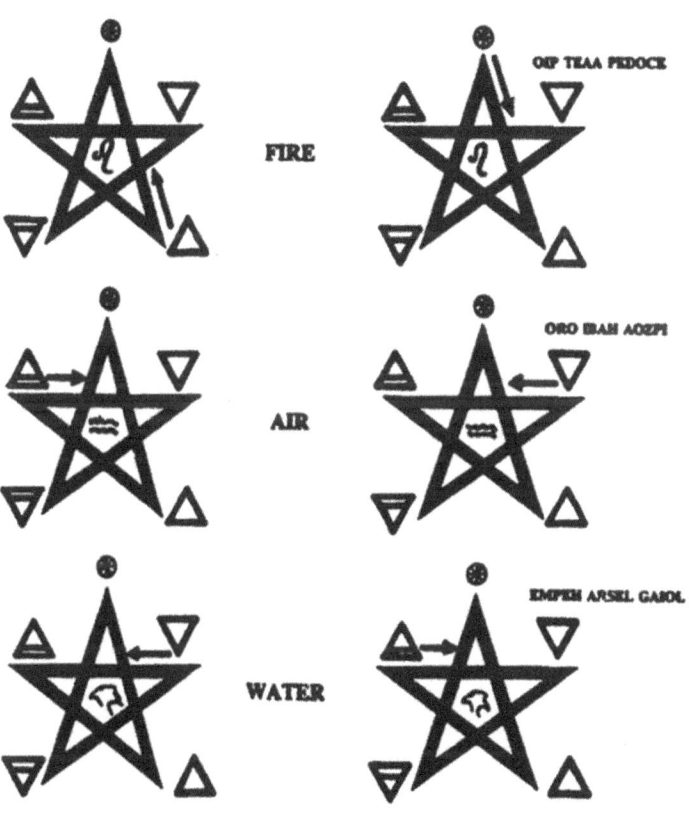

**Signs Of The Grades
Diagram I**

Diagram I

Appendix III
The Lesser Rituals of the Pentagram and Hexagram

THE LESSER RITUAL OF THE PENTAGRAM

(i) Touching the forehead, say Ateh (Unto Thee).
(ii) Touching the breast, say Malkuth (The Kingdom).
(iii) Touching the right shoulder, say ve-Geburah (and the Power).
(iv) Touching the left shoulder, say ve-Gedulah (and the Glory).
(v) Clasping the hands upon the breast, say le-Olahm, Amen (to the Ages, Amen).
(vi) Turning to the East, make a Pentagram (that of Earth) with the proper weapon (usually the Wand). Say (*i.e.*, vibrate) I H V H.
(vii) Turning to the South, the same, but say A D N I.
(viii) Turning to the West, the same, but say A H I H.
(ix) Turning to the North, the same, but say A G L A.
(x) Extending the arms in the form of a Cross, say:
(xi) Before me Raphael;
(xii) Behind me Gabriel;
(xiii) On my right hand Michael;
(xiv) On my left hand Auriel;
(xv) For about me flames the Pentagram;
(xvi) And in the Column shines the six-rayed Star.
(xvii-xxi) Repeat (i) to (v), the "Qabalistic Cross."

THE LESSER RITUAL OF THE HEXAGRAM

This ritual operates upon the Macrocosm in the same manner that the Pentagram ritual operates upon the Microcosm. It is to be performed after the "Lesser Ritual of the Pentagram" and is most appropriate for the invocations of the Enochian Seniors.

1. Stand upright, feet together, left arm at side, right arm across body, holding the wand or other weapon upright in the median line. Then face East, and say:

2. "I.N.R.I.
   Yod. Nun. Resh. Yod.
   Virgo, Isis, Mighty Mother.
   Scorpio, Apophis, Destroyer.
   Sol, Osiris, Slain and Risen.
   Isis, Apophris, Osiris, IAO."

3. Extend the arms in the form of a cross, and say:

"The sign of Osiris Slain." (See illustration.)

4. Raise the right arm to point upwards, keeping the elbow square, and lower the left arm to point downwards, keeping the elbow square, while turning the head over the left shoulder looking down so that the eyes follow the left forearm, and say:

"The sign of the Mourning of Isis" (See illustration.)

5. Raise the arms at an angle of sixty degrees to each other above the head, which is thrown back, and say:

"The sign of Apophis and Typhon." (See illustration.)

6. Cross the arms on the breast, bow the head, and say:

"The sign of Osiris Risen." (See illustration.)

7. Extend the arms again as in (3) and cross them again as in (6) saying:

"L.V.X. Lux, the Light of the Cross."

8. With the magical weapon trace the Hexagram of Fire in the East, saying: "ARARITA."

(This is a word created by the initials

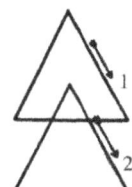

of a Hebrew sentence which means "One is His Beginning: One is His Individuality: His Permutation is One.")

This Hexagram consists of two equilateral triangles, both apices pointing upwards. Begin at the top of the upper triangle and trace it in a clockwise direction. The top of the lower triangle should coincide with the central point of the upper triangle.

9. Turn to the South.
Trace the Hexagram of Earth
saying: "ARARITA."

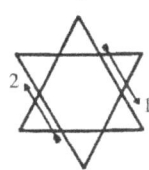

(This Hexagram has the apex of the lower triangle pointing downwards, and it should be capable of inscription in a circle.

10. Turn to the West.
Trace the Hexagram of Air
saying: "ARARITA."

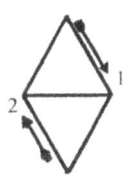

(This Hexagram is like that of the Earth: but the bases of the triangles coincide, forming a diamond.

11. Turn to the North.
Trace the Hexagram of Water
saying: "ARARITA."

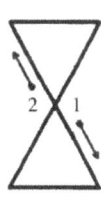

(This Hexagram has the lower triangle placed above the upper, so that their apices coincide.

12. Return to the East and repeat steps (1-7).

The Banishing Ritual is identical, save that the direction of the Hexagrams must be reversed.

To invoke or banish Planets or Zodiacal signs, the Hexagram of Earth alone is used. Draw the Hexagram, beginning from the point which is attributed to the planet you are dealing with.

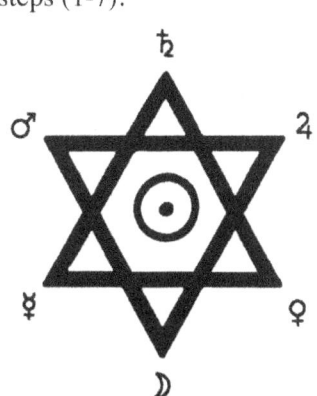

SEX MAGICK SYMBOLS

**The Lovers
Divine and Elemental**

Babalon And The Beast Conjoined

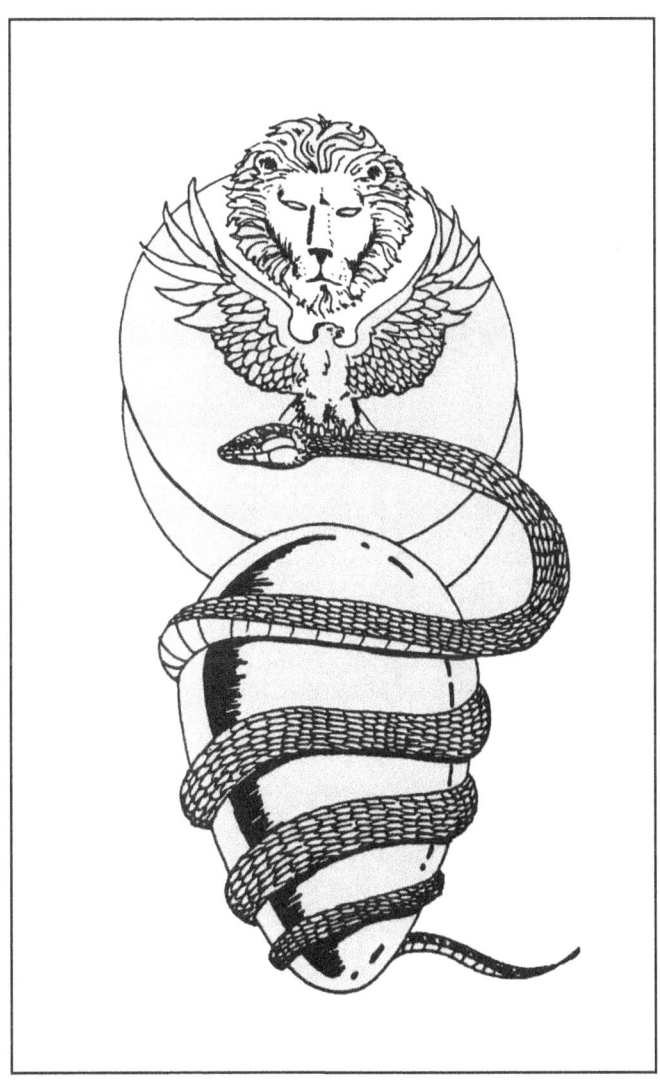

The Quintessence Of Sexual Alchemy

**The Charging Of The Seed
Through Concentrated Will**

The Holy Graal
The Creation Of The Elixir Of Life

**The Annihilation Of The Ego
In The Thunder Orgasm**

**The Orgastic Circulation Of Light
The Supreme Attainment**

**The Lingam and Yoni
Western Tantric Symbolism**

Pattern for Enochian Square Truncated Pyramid

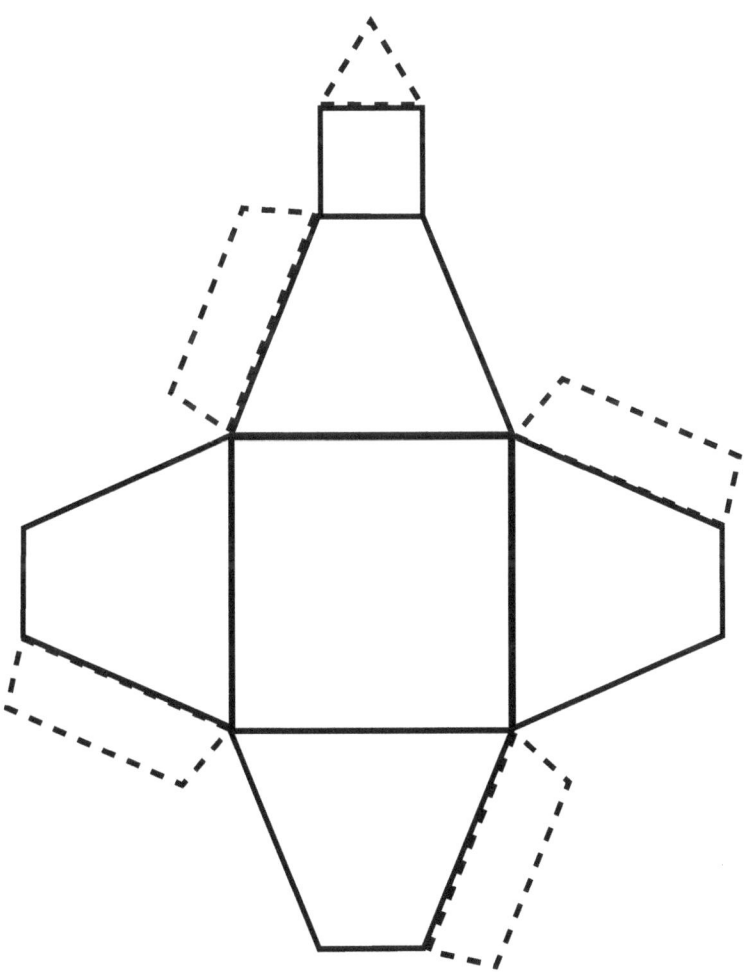

New Falcon Publications
**Publisher of Controversial Books and CDs
Invites You to Visit Our Website:
http://www.newfalcon.com**

At the Falcon website you can:

- Browse the online catalog of all our great titles, including books by Robert Anton Wilson, Christopher S. Hyatt, Israel Regardie, Aleister Crowley, Timothy Leary, Osho, Lon Milo DuQuette and many more
- Find out what's available and what's out of stock
- Get special discounts
- Order our titles through our secure online server
- Find products not available anywhere else including:
    – One of a kind and limited availability products
    – Special packages
    – Special pricing
- And much, much more

Get online today at http://www.newfalcon.com